Nuclear Power

THE STUDY OF QUARKS AND SPARKS

J. S. Kidd and Renee A. Kidd

CHELSEA HOUSE
PUBLISHERS
An imprint of Infobase Publishing

This one is for Jim Liesener, who maintained the faith
and would—if he could—make sure that every
media center, school library, and public library in
this country and abroad was stocked with good books.

♦

Nuclear Power: The Study of Quarks and Sparks

Copyright © 2006 by J. S. Kidd and Renee A. Kidd

This is a revised edition of QUARKS AND SPARKS: The Story of Nuclear Power
Copyright © 1999 by J. S. Kidd and Renee A. Kidd

Chelsea House
An imprint of Infobase Publishing
132 West 31st Street
New York NY 10001

Library of Congress Cataloging-in-Publication Data

Kidd, J. S. (Jerry S.)
    Nuclear power : the study of quarks and sparks / J. S. Kidd and Renee A. Kidd.
    p. cm.
    Rev. ed. of: Quarks and sparks. 1999.
    Includes bibliographical references and index.
    ISBN 0-8160-5606-4 (acid-free paper)
    1. Nuclear energy—Juvenile literature. I. Kidd, Renee A. II. Kidd, J. S. (Jerry
S.) Quarks and sparks. III. Title.

    QC792.5.K53 2006
    621.48—dc22   2005052872

Chelsea House books are available at special discounts when purchased in bulk
quantities for businesses, associations, institutions, or sales promotions. Please call
our Special Sales Department in New York at (212) 967-8800 or (800) 322-8755.

You can find Chelsea House on the World Wide Web at http://www.chelseahouse.com

Text design by James Scotto-Lavino
Cover design by Pehrsson Design
Illustrations by Sholto Ainslie

Printed in the United States of America

MP FOF 10 9 8 7 6 5 4 3 2 1

This book is printed on acid-free paper.

Contents

Preface

The products of science and technology influence the lives of all citizens, including young adults. New means of communication and transportation, new ways of doing work and pursuing recreation, new foods and new medicines arrive almost daily. Science also engenders new ways of looking at the world and at other citizens. Likewise, science can raise concerns about moral and ethical values.

Dealing with all such changes requires some resiliency. The needed adaptations by individuals are fostered by knowledge of the inner workings of science and technology and of the researchers and engineers who do the studies and design the products. Consequently, one of the goals of the Science and Society set of books is to illuminate these subjects in a way that is both accurate and understandable.

One of the obstacles in reaching that goal is the fact that almost all the connections between citizens and scientists are impersonal. For example, the direction of study in a specialized field of science is now mainly determined by negotiations between the leaders of research projects and government officials. National elections rarely hinge on questions of science and technology. Such matters are usually relegated to secondary political status. In any case, most of the officials who are concerned with science are not elected but are appointed and are members of large government bureaucracies.

Other influences on the directions taken by science and technology come from other bureaucratic organizations, such as international political bodies, large commercial firms, academic institutions, or philanthropic foundations. However, in recent years, influence has also come from more informal voluntary groups of citizens and citizen action organizations. The scope of the set has been revised to reflect the growing importance of such channels linking citizens to the leaders in science.

The books describe some of the dramatic adventures on the part of the people who do scientific work, show the human side of science, and convey the idea that scientists experience the same kinds of day-to-day frustrations that afflict everyone.

The revisions attempt to show some of the developing trends in the impact of science on sections of the citizenry such as groupings by age or gender—or geographic location. An example is the change in the living conditions in small, rural communities that have come about as a consequence of agricultural mechanization. Finally, the books describe some of the significant strides in the actual findings of science in recent years. Some fields of science such as genetics and molecular biology have gone through a virtual revolution. These radical changes are ongoing. Likewise, the development of natural medicines was recently given social prominence by the establishment of government agencies devoted explicitly to the support of such research.

Science and Society shows the extent to which individuals can have a stake in the enterprise called science and technology—how they can cope with the societal changes entailed and how they can exert some personal influence on what is happening.

Acknowledgments

A nne Mavor, James McGee, and Susan McCutchen at the Commission on the Behavioral and Social Sciences and Education of the National Research Council and Diane Barlow and others at the College of Information Studies at the University of Maryland, College Park, were supportive as usual. In addition, we must cite Joseph and Stephanie Gonyeau for their responsiveness to some questions about nuclear power in general and propulsion systems in particular.

Introduction

This book is about the forces that hold the universe together. It describes the work of some of the scientists, most of them physicists, who have tried to understand these forces. It also covers some aspects of the role of the public and elected officials in supporting or opposing such work. It is about nuclear power.

About 2,500 years ago, Greek philosophers speculated that the world was composed of very small, indivisible, and indestructible units of matter. The ancient scholars called these units *atomos*. Over the centuries, learned people continued to consider this idea but did not attempt to prove or disprove the concept. Indeed, significant scientific advances in this area did not begin to occur until about 200 years ago. Then, after a slow beginning, the field of atomic science grew rapidly during the 1900s. The science of atoms now includes explanations for commonplace things, such as the flash of lightning, and exotic phenomena, such as quarks.

The public and people in governments ignored the first important advances in atomic research. When breakthroughs became more highly publicized, some of the results were treated as a form of entertainment. In the late 1800s, for example, X-rays were discovered as a result of atomic studies. Scientists realized immediately that X-rays would be invaluable in medicine and research; however, some people viewed this technology as a novelty or a device to penetrate a person's privacy.

Until the 1930s, little atomic research was done in the United States. Most physicists worked in European laboratories.

At first, their projects were relatively simple. Teachers conducted much of the research in their spare time. They used inexpensive and often homemade apparatus. Most of the modest financial support for their work came from private, philanthropic sources. Government funding was rare.

In the late 1930s, calculations based on early atomic studies revealed that nuclear weapons were possible. A major war was looming, and many government officials suddenly became interested in atomic research. Subsequent studies proved the theories were correct, and scientists were persuaded to design, build, and test atomic weaponry. Governments, not private sources, moved to finance this undertaking. New government agencies were founded to channel funds into scientific research and weapons development. One result was the atomic bombs that helped bring World War II to a close.

The public was not involved, either directly or indirectly through their elected representatives, in the decisions concerning nuclear weapons. Even after the end of World War II, ordinary citizens knew little about weapon development or other applications of nuclear energy. Such work was carried out in secret in the interests of national security by those governments that had nuclear capabilities. Decisions on other related issues of great public concern—such as using nuclear materials in medicine—continued to be made with little public participation.

Then, in the 1950s—while the cold war world worried about a nuclear war—the government of the United States established a program called Atoms for Peace. This and other similar plans provided the public with some information on nuclear energy. Public discussions, however, were rare, and public influence on policy decisions was still limited.

More than 20 years later, government policies changed forever when situations such as the emergency shutdown of the nuclear reactor at Three Mile Island near Harrisburg, Pennsylvania, received international news coverage. Likewise, the mass media have disclosed many of the technical details of weapon design and the hazards of radiation exposure. Today, the public is far better informed on all facets of atomic research and development. Citizens are encouraged to participate in open discussions on problems of the nuclear age.

Although the threat of nuclear war has declined in recent years, the public continues to be deeply concerned with nuclear energy and atomic research. Many people are skeptical about the policies and agencies that control and regulate the construction and operation of nuclear power plants. The reclamation of areas contaminated by atomic waste, the storage of atomic waste products, and the safety of nuclear power plants are prominent issues. The funding of costly and sophisticated equipment to further atomic research has also become an important consideration.

Unfortunately, many politicians and scientists still regard nuclear science as too exotic and complicated for public understanding. Others believe that the public is too uninterested or uninformed to participate in decisions about the utilization of nuclear energy. This book is intended to help dispel such views on the politician's and scientist's part as well as some of the fears and misunderstandings in the general public's mind due to a lack of information.

Advances have been made in the basic science behind nuclear energy. As a result, our understanding of subatomic particles has been extended. Specifically, scientists can now identify more than 100 different subatomic particles. The number rises above 200 if antiparticles are taken into consideration. The researchers are also able to understand what roles these particles play in the structure of the material universe: For example, they can now connect particle attributes to stages in the evolution of the cosmos. The forces between particles will dictate the fate of the universe in the far-distant future.

On the practical side, the full therapeutic and diagnostic promise of medical isotopes is at last being realized. Likewise, the use of high-energy particles can reveal the inner structure of the materials used to make consumer products. This technology has moved ahead rapidly and could bridge the gap between physics and biology by allowing biologists to make superfine analyses of the molecules in the genome that are as complicated as strands of RNA.

There is still much that is unknown. For instance, the dynamics of mass/energy transformations are still unknown. In a similar vein, the geometry of space/time is still mysterious. Some theoreticians suggest that there are many more dimensions in space/time than the four with which we are familiar. If true, there might be still more particles to be found.

1

Preparing the Ground

In the fifth century B.C., the Greek philosopher Democritus and a few of his successors maintained that all matter was composed of very small hard atoms. An atom—from the Greek word for indivisible—was thought to be invisible, unchangeable, and indestructible. The logic by which the philosophers arrived at this theory is not known. Possibly they saw that dense matter such as rock could be broken into smaller and smaller pieces. They might have speculated that the smallest pieces could be broken down still further until they became invisible.

Through the ages, scholars believed that substances differed from one another in appearance, taste, or odor because their atoms were organized in different ways. They may have compared atoms to building materials such as stones that could be used to build many different structures—huts, fences, or beautiful palaces.

In a broad sense, the ancient notion was correct because atoms are the building blocks of all matter. However, for many centuries, the concept of the atom was not a true scientific theory. A scientific theory must be testable by experimentation or by other means of observation. Early philosophers and scholars had no reliable instruments or methods to conduct the necessary scientific investigations.

Nevertheless, learned people did not dismiss Democritus's theory. As an abstract or untested idea, it continued to appear in the writings of European thinkers. During ancient Roman times, the poet and philosopher Lucretius wrote about the idea. Philippus Paracelsus, a 16th-century Swiss physician, agreed with the ancient philosophy. In the 17th century, Isaac Newton, the founder of modern physics, incorporated the notion of atoms in some of his writings, but his great studies on the orbits of the planets and the properties of light did not include this theory.

True Research Begins

Electricity was one of the first important subjects of scientific research. This force had been a source of puzzlement to people for many generations. Early people knew that pieces of amber— a beautiful, highly prized material made of petrified tree resin— had an unusual and unexplained property. After amber rods were rubbed with cloth, the rods would attract small pieces of dust or other substances. The ancients named this property *elektron,* the Greek word for amber. Today, the same type of crackles and clinging that result from static electricity can be experienced when combing one's hair, taking articles from a clothes dryer, or walking across a carpet made of artificial fibers.

Ancient peoples also knew of magnetism. Magnetism is the ability of certain materials, such as lodestone, to attract iron and other metals such as nickel. The word *magnetism* is taken from the name of the ancient Greek region of Magnesia where lodestone was found. Similarly, ancient peoples were alert to the power of lightning, but its connection with static electricity was not established until the mid-1700s.

By the middle of the 18th century and during the 19th century, new fields of scientific studies were rapidly evolving. For example, in 1745, the Dutch scientist Pieter van Musschenbroek aided the study of electricity by inventing the Leyden jar, a device that allowed the collection and storage of static electricity. The Leyden jar worked so well that the touch of a human hand could discharge sufficient electrical energy to knock a person down. Both the inside and outside of the jar are lined with metal foil. Static electricity is conducted to the inner lining by a wire inserted through a rubber stopper. After a charge has accumulated, the wire is touched to the outer lining to discharge the stored electricity.

In America, Benjamin Franklin began studies of electric currents that led to his kite experiment in 1752. It is said that Franklin was the first to use the terms positive and negative to describe one of the properties of an electric charge.

In 1771, the Italian physiologist Luigi Galvani discovered that the leg of a dead frog would jerk when touched by wire carrying an electric current. Such a current could be generated by certain chemical reactions. His research was expanded by another Italian, Count Alessandro Volta, 30 years later. Galvani's work led Volta, a physicist, to the invention of the electric storage battery.

French scientist Charles-Augustin de Coulomb confirmed in 1782 that an electric current has two poles, or terminals, one positive and one negative. His studies revealed that two like poles repel each other and two unlike poles attract each other. These findings verified Franklin's observations. In addition, Coulomb observed that the ability of the poles to attract or repel each other declined as they were moved farther apart. After more study, he realized that these effects were similar to the attraction and repulsion between the like and unlike poles of a magnet. Coulomb's studies gave the first hint that electricity and magnetism might be closely related.

In 1807, the Danish physicist Hans Christian Ørsted set out to prove Coulomb's theory of a connection between electricity and magnetism. He found his proof in 1819 when he discovered that an electric current changes the position of the needle of a magnetic compass. This observation supported the idea that electricity and magnetism are connected. Their connection is known as *electromagnetism.*

Soon scientists including André-Marie Ampère, a French mathematician and physicist, were working on similar projects. Building on Ørsted's discovery, Ampère proved that electric currents, like magnets, can attract or repel each other. He also demonstrated that an electric current, like a magnetic force field, can attract iron filings. Over the years, the names of many important chemists and physicists have entered our everyday vocabulary as words pertaining to the workings of electricity: *ampere* or *amp* are named for Ampère; *coulomb,* for Coulomb; *volt,* for Volta.

Chemistry Moves Forward in Parallel

The English chemist John Dalton is recognized as the founder of modern atomic theory. Dalton was born in 1766 into the family of a poor weaver in a small village in northern England. The Dalton family belonged to a large Quaker community whose members were deeply concerned about the importance of education, hard work, and morality.

Dalton attended a small local school until he was 11 years old. The next year, the teacher retired, and the 12-year-old John Dalton was given his job. At first, Dalton taught the students in his own home, but he soon moved the class into the local Quaker meetinghouse. Three years later, Dalton joined some relatives to teach and study at another Quaker school about 40 miles from his home. He was then 15 years old.

Dalton's own education was furthered by a slightly older teacher at the school, John Gough. Gough, a brilliant scholar and fellow Quaker, was totally blind. Dalton's future scientific research was greatly influenced by this remarkable man.

In 1793, Gough helped Dalton obtain a position as a teacher of mathematics and natural philosophy in Manchester, England. In those days, natural philosophy referred to the complete field of science. When the school moved in 1799,

Dalton decided to stay in Manchester and accept private pupils. Again, the Quaker community came to his aid. They offered him a large room in their meetinghouse to serve as his study, classroom, and research laboratory. At last, Dalton had the time and the space to carry out his own investigations.

The 26-year-old Dalton soon published the first of many scientific writings and began his careful experiments on the little-understood characteristics of gases. By 1803, he reintroduced the idea of the atom. He was particularly curious about why water absorbs some gases more easily than others. His investigations led to the idea that the atoms composing one gas might be larger than those of another gas. He concluded that small particles would be more easily absorbed by the water than large ones would. Dalton wanted to know whether the larger units were different in other ways as well. Continuing his research, he discovered that a variety of chemical properties varied in conjunction with what he supposed to be the size of the atoms. Dalton's work persuaded him that all atoms were not identical. He came to believe that each chemical element such as carbon or oxygen was composed of a different kind of atom.

Other chemists found that when certain compounds, such as water (H_2O), were broken down into their separate elements, the proportionate weight of each of the separated parts was always the same. For example, when water was broken down into oxygen and hydrogen, the weight of oxygen is always eight times the weight of hydrogen. This and other observations suggested that the ancient idea that all atoms were identical was wrong.

Back to Physics

Chemists such as Dalton continued to identify the elements that made up all substances and investigate the processes by

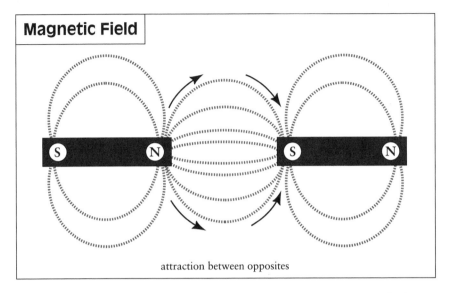

Magnetic Field

attraction between opposites

The pattern that iron filings make around two bar magnets reveals the presence of an invisible magnetic field.

which these substances were formed. Physicists, on the other hand, continued their research on electricity.

In 1831, the independent research of an Englishman, Michael Faraday, and an American, Joseph Henry, demonstrated that electricity can be generated by rotating a coil of wire between the poles of a U-shaped stationary magnet. Faraday later made another important discovery while studying the effect of a magnet on a collection of iron filings. The filings, randomly scattered over a piece of paper, moved into a definite formation when placed over a bar magnet. Although the ability of a magnet to attract iron filings had been known for centuries, Faraday was able to explain the reason for this phenomenon. The formation of the filings showed the shape of the usually invisible force field around the magnet.

In 1845, Faraday saw that light was a form of energy as when sunlight is concentrated by a magnifying glass to generate heat. He proposed that light was a form of electromagnetic radiation. This was the first step in identifying the whole range of electromagnetic properties associated with radiation. By 1873, the Scottish physicist James Clerk Maxwell had identified the invisible rays in the infrared and ultraviolet ranges of light. Maxwell's research proved that infrared was light at a lower frequency than visible light and that ultraviolet was light at a higher frequency than visible light. German physicist Heinrich Rudolf Hertz used Maxwell's ideas in 1888 to produce much lower frequency electromagnetic waves. They were the first radio waves.

In the continuing attempts to understand the basic nature of electricity, many physicists became interested in studying the flow of electricity in a vacuum. At this time in the late 1800s, scientists believed that all electric currents had to be carried by something, such as air or water. A vacuum is a void, yet the transmission of electricity in a vacuum could easily be observed. In order to further investigate this apparent paradox, almost every physics laboratory included a cathode-ray tube. A vacuum can be created in this special glass cylinder when all or most of the air is pumped out. The first tubes were about one to two feet (30 to 60 cm) long with electric contacts (pieces of bare metal) embedded in the glass at each end. To study the flow of electricity, a wire from the negative pole of an electric storage battery was attached to the contact on one end, and a wire from the positive pole of the battery was attached to the contact at the other end. Inside the tube, a stream of electricity, called a cathode ray, would jump the gap between the contact points and flow from one end of the tube to the other. If any gas remained in the tube, the cathode rays would be seen as colored light. Colors would also be seen in the glass of the cathode-ray tube. This occurred when the rays struck the tube near the anode (the positive contact point). The variety of colors depended on the materials of which the glass tube was made.

Toward the end of the 1800s, the research on atomic theory begun by chemists such as Dalton and the studies on radiation and electricity done by physicists such as Maxwell were brought together into one field. This merger was very fruitful; indeed, a golden age of atomic research was beginning. Between 1890 and 1940, knowledge about the structure of atoms grew rapidly.

Some Lucky Breaks

Two accidental discoveries helped set the pace. The first occurred in 1895. The German physicist Wilhelm Conrad Röntgen (or Roentgen), like many physicists of his time, was experimenting with the radiation that comes from a cathode-ray tube. During one study, he had covered the tube with black paper to prevent any light from escaping. When he activated his equipment in a fully darkened room, he saw that a panel placed some distance from the tube began to sparkle. Röntgen remembered that the panel had been painted with a phospho-

Early Cathode-Ray Tube

cathode

anode

sparkles of light

valve for vacuum pump

switch

electrical power source

An early version of a cathode-ray tube.

rescent compound as part of a different experiment. He speculated that the radiation from the cathode-ray tube was causing this strange occurrence. When he tried to block the path of radiation by using nearby objects made of wood or metal, Röntgen found that a piece of thick metal could obstruct the rays. When Röntgen placed his hand in front of the glowing panel, he discovered something truly amazing. He could see a rough image of his hand bones on the phosphorescent panel. Although the full scientific explanation of this phenomenon was not known, fellow scientists quickly realized the possible medical applications. Because X is the mathematical notation for an unknown, the rays that Röntgen discovered were known as X-rays. Later it would be observed that natural atomic radiation contained the same kind of rays.

Wilhelm Röntgen, a young German professor of physics, conducted a series of experiments after his accidental discovery of X-rays in order to be certain of his findings. (Courtesy of the National Library of Medicine)

Röntgen and other scientists conducted many experiments with X-rays. They soon demonstrated that these rays were not influenced by magnetism or electric currents. These facts established that X-rays were in the same family as visible and invisible light.

The ability to generate and focus X-rays quickly improved, and they were used in medicine to detect bone fractures. X-ray machines became so common that they were used in shoe stores to assure proper fitting shoes. Amusement parks used them to reveal the contents of patrons' pockets. No one understood the hazards of X-ray exposure.

In 1896, the French physicist Antoine-Henri Becquerel made a startling discovery. He had become interested in the physical properties of heavy metals such as lead. For his research, Bequerel had obtained a small lump of uranium oxide. He wrapped the uranium sample in a piece of black cloth and casually placed it and some unexposed photographic film in the same desk drawer. When he opened the drawer some time later, the film showed evidence of having been exposed. Becquerel deduced that the only source of energy that could have exposed the film was the uranium. Quite by accident, he had found that natural atomic radiation comes from the element uranium.

Further observation showed that rays from uranium, like X-rays, are invisible and reveal their presence when they strike a phosphorescent material that then gives off sparks. After a series of experiments, Becquerel determined that rays from uranium can penetrate many different opaque materials. In this respect, too, these rays are similar to X-rays.

The next important investigations were directly focused on atomic research. These studies soon dispelled the ancient idea that the atom was a solid object.

The Nuclear Pioneers

JOSEPH JOHN THOMSON

In 1897, Joseph John Thomson, an English physicist, was working with cathode-rays in his laboratory at Cambridge University. He hoped to build on earlier experiments that had revealed the electrical properties of atoms. Specifically, these investigations had shown that atoms of some elements could acquire a negative electrical charge while atoms of other elements could have a positive electrical charge. In order to uncover more basic information about this phenomenon, he planned a series of studies. Thomson knew that the negatively charged cathode at one end of the tube repelled the particles that made up the cathode ray and that the positively charged anode at the other end attracted them. Scientists knew that like charges repel each other and unlike charges attract. Therefore, after several experiments, Thomson proposed that the ray itself was composed of negatively charged matter.

Thomson then devised a clever way to determine the weight of the invisible particles streaming from the cathode to the anode. He installed two electrically charged plates in his cathode-ray tube. One plate was placed just above the stream of cathode rays and the other just below it. Thomson was able to change the strength of the charge by adjusting the amount of electricity at the plates. As he modified the charge, he measured the extent to which the rays were bent. By using a complicated mathematical formula, he calculated the amount of electrical force required to alter the path of the substance that makes up the cathode rays. Because the amount of force necessary to change the substance is related to the weight of the substance, Thomson could estimate the weight of the particles in the cathode ray. This weight was exceedingly small—only about $1/2000$ the weight of the lightest atom, hydrogen.

The idea of the "electron" had been developing for 100 years or more and the name had been given to the material flow in a cathode-ray tube as early as 1855. With Thomson's discovery of the electrons' weight, however, scientists were surprised that these objects were so small. In reaction to this surprise, another idea appeared: Perhaps atoms were not altogether hard and solid; perhaps they were assemblies of even smaller units.

MARIE AND PIERRE CURIE

Before the 20th century, few women were involved in the study of biology, chemistry, mathematics, or other scientific fields. Many schools of higher learning would not accept women students in any science department. Today, women are teachers and researchers in all areas of science. The path of women in science was first marked by Marie Curie.

Marie Curie was born Manya Skłodowska in 1867 in Warsaw, Poland. She was the fifth child of two teachers. Maria's father taught physics and mathematics. Her mother was an accomplished musician and taught in a girl's school. The family was far from wealthy. Poland at that time was ruled by Russia, and Russian, rather than Polish, teachers were given the best positions in all levels of education.

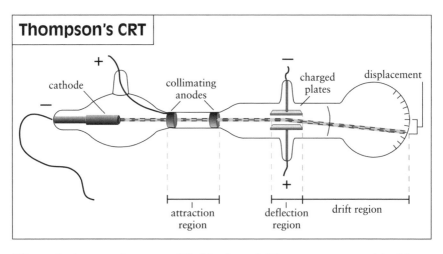

The cathode-ray tube, as modified by Joseph Thomson, was used by him to determine the electrical charge of electrons (beta particles). The ring-shaped anodes attract electrons and force them into a narrow stream. Once the stream of electrons passes the positively charged anodes, the electrons are said to drift. When they pass near a charged plate, they are displaced. The amount of deflection is correlated with their mass.

When Maria was 11, her mother died of tuberculosis. At age 15, Maria graduated from high school. She wanted to continue her studies at a Polish university; however, the political situation in Poland and the ban on women students by Polish universities made her ambition impossible to realize.

For a brief period, she spent her free time taking courses at a "floating university" in Warsaw. Because the school was not authorized by the Russian government, the teachers and students were involved in an illegal activity. The secret police hated such institutions. They realized that the schools were centers of antigovernment sentiment and potential subversion. The classes were therefore conducted in any space that seemed safe from spies, and they "floated" from one building to another. Of course, this type of education was not ideal.

Maria's older sister Bronya was able to go to Paris to study medicine at the Sorbonne. At that time, many young Poles continued their university training in France. The French government was hospitable to Polish immigrants because of historic ties that had existed before the Russian takeover of Poland.

Bronya was able to pay her expenses by tutoring some private students. When Maria was 17, she resolved to earn enough money to follow Bronya to Paris. From 1885 until 1891, she worked as a governess and eventually saved enough money to go to Paris. There, she lived with few comforts but was able to earn two master's degrees, one in science and one in mathematics, from the Sorbonne in 1892 and 1893.

One of her professors recommended her for a temporary research position at the School of Physics and Chemistry of the City of Paris. She met Pierre Curie there in 1894. Pierre's father and grandfather were notable physicians; however, both he and his brother, Jacques, chose science rather than medicine for their careers.

While still a student, Pierre did some pioneering research on the connection between the physics of metals and electricity

Pierre Curie, Marie Skłodowska Curie, and their daughter, Irene. Marie, by isolating radium and polonium, proved that radioactivity was a property shared by several minerals. (Courtesy of the National Library of Medicine)

by showing that some types of metallic crystals give off an electric charge when put under physical pressure. After graduation, Pierre went into the study of magnetism. He was hired as a teacher and researcher by a new institution, the School of Physics and Chemistry in Paris. He was working there in rather impoverished circumstances when he and Maria met.

Coincidentally, Maria was working on a project directed at the magnetic properties of tempered steel at this time. Their scientific interests merged with their personal interests, and they married in 1895. Maria became Marie Curie.

The young couple lived frugally in a small apartment. Marie was allowed to use a room in Pierre's college to finish the necessary experiments to gain a teaching certificate. Two years after their marriage, their daughter Irène was born. Years later, this daughter would also become a prominent physicist.

Shortly after Irène's birth, Marie decided to begin working toward her doctorate in science. At that time, no European woman had been granted a doctoral degree, and the young couple understood the difficulties that they would face. However, Pierre's mother had recently died, and his father, now retired, was free to care for baby Irène while the parents worked and studied.

Marie soon faced the problem of finding a topic for her independent research project. She had been fascinated by the initial findings of Becquerel and set out to increase her understanding of the rays he had discovered in 1896.

Uranium was known to be the source of these rays, but there were many strange inconsistencies in the measurements of the strength of the rays. For example, the intensity of the rays might decline after a period of strong activity. Then, activity would be restored for no apparent reason. Also, uranium ore was more active than purified uranium metal. It occurred to Pierre and Marie Curie that there might be more than one element giving off radiation. Some of the peculiar measurements could be explained if a mixture of elements of differing radioactive strength were mixed in with the uranium.

Marie obtained several hundred pounds of tailings, the residue of uranium refinement, from an Australian mining company and began the laborious process of re-refining this ore in search of a trace of a new element. The chemical extraction techniques used by the Curies had been designed to isolate the element bismuth along with any heavy metal from low-grade ore. The process was very laborious. After several months of work, they were able to isolate the small amount of bismuth that had been in the ore. In the chemical reaction, the bismuth carried with it another metal of previously unknown properties. This other metal had never been isolated before. It had stronger radioactivity than pure uranium. The Curies named the new metal polonium in honor of Marie's home country.

Another chemical process separated barium from the ore, and together with the barium came still another new metal that was thousands of times more active than pure uranium. It took Marie until 1902 to isolate $1/_{10}$ of a gram of this material, but that was enough to prove that it had a distinctive atomic weight and other unique chemical features. The Curies called this new material radium.

There was still one more new element hidden in the ore. It was extracted the following year by a young partner working with the Curies named André Debierne. His find was called actinium, the Greek equivalent to the Latin *radium.*

In addition to the search for new elements, the Curies and other researchers were avidly studying the odd nature of the radiation that came from heavy metals. In the last years of the 1800s, Ernest Rutherford was among those who sought the solution to this puzzle.

ERNEST RUTHERFORD'S CONTRIBUTIONS

Rutherford was born in New Zealand and showed the intensity and adventuresome spirit common to many of the British Empire's settlers in faraway lands. After completing his formal studies at Cambridge under J. J. Thomson, he accepted a position at McGill University in Montreal, Canada. Rutherford did not want merely to continue research in Thomson's field of cathode rays. Instead, he decided to study the recently discovered rays emanating from radioactive elements such as uranium.

In 1899, Rutherford discovered two types of such radiation. He named these strange rays *alpha* and *beta* from the first two letters of the Greek alphabet. Experiments showed that some alpha rays could penetrate a glass wall but seemed to be stopped by metal foil or even by a piece of paper. On the other hand, beta rays could penetrate much thicker foil. In 1902, beta rays were proven to be the electrons discovered by Rutherford's teacher, Thomson. A third type of ray was detected in 1903 and named *gamma,* the third letter of the Greek alphabet. This ray could pass through a metal shield and proved to be similar to the X-rays discovered earlier by Röntgen.

In 1905, Rutherford and a colleague, English physicist Frederick Soddy, discovered that portions of the radioactive element thorium spontaneously changed into a different element. They began to formulate a theory on the disintegration of radioactive elements. The theory states that the breakdown of the heavy metal uranium—and other such elements—occurs when the nuclei of uranium atoms emit radiation in the form of particles. These particles form other, lighter elements such as helium.

While still at McGill, Rutherford designed an experiment that revealed some of the properties of the newly discovered alpha particles. A sample of uranium was put in a glass container and placed next to a tightly sealed glass tube from which all air had been removed. Since the alpha particles coming from uranium are energetic, some passed from the original container into the adjacent tube. After a few days, Rutherford analyzed the contents of the second tube and found traces of the element helium. The only way that helium could have come into the tube was by means of the alpha radiation. Rutherford reasoned that the alpha particles were the nuclei of helium atoms that were split from the uranium during the process of disintegration (or radioactive decay). Rutherford won the Nobel Prize in physics in 1908 for this work.

Uranium into Thorium 234

alpha particle

• protons
○ neutrons

Schematic diagram of uranium emitting an alpha particle consisting of two protons and two neutrons—the same as a helium nucleus.

Another of Rutherford and Soddy's experiments focused on the observation that samples of radium always include trace amounts of polonium and lead. They also noticed that radium appears to emit a radioactive gas called radon. The two scientists set out to comprehend these interesting phenomena. After careful research, they suggested that radium was actually being transformed into radon. Later, they understood that this transformation was the first stage of an extended process. When radium loses two helium nuclei by natural radioactivity, it is transformed into radon. When radon loses six helium nuclei, it turns into polonium. In the last stage of the process, polonium loses two helium nuclei and becomes lead. Lead is a stable substance and will not break down into another element. By using a formula based on his observations of the transformation process, Rutherford calculated that half of a given amount of radium would become lead in 1,620 years. This number of years is known as the *half-life* of radium.

Other scientists observed that radioactive materials disintegrate at different speeds. Thorium, for example, breaks down at a very slow rate: It has a half-life of 13 billion years.

2
The Atom

While still at McGill University, Ernest Rutherford and Frederick Soddy demonstrated another instance of the transformation of one element into another. Using uranium as a source of alpha particles and using a container with an opening like the barrel of a gun to focus a stream of particles, the two scientists began to bombard a variety of materials. One of these materials was pure nitrogen gas in a glass container. From their previous studies, Rutherford and Soddy believed that some of the alpha particles would penetrate the glass and would strike the nuclei of the nitrogen atoms. This belief was confirmed when the contents of the glass container were analyzed after a long period of exposure to the alpha radiation. The analysis showed that there was now a trace of oxygen present. They explained this discovery by suggesting that when a collision between the particles and the nuclei happened, one proton and two neutral particles from the alpha radiation were absorbed by some of the nitrogen atoms. Consequently, the nitrogen nuclei that were struck by alpha particles gained three units of weight and one unit of positive charge. The addition of one unit of positive charge meant that the former nitrogen atom now had the same charge as an oxygen atom. The added weight also made it resemble an oxygen atom. Indeed, some of the nitrogen had been transformed into oxygen.

Soddy went on to formulate the idea of isotopes, based in part on the results of the nitrogen-to-oxygen transformation.

His tests had revealed that the weight of the resultant oxygen atom was slightly different from the weight of normal oxygen—it was heavier. It weighed 17 units rather than the 16 units characteristic of normal oxygen, yet it was clearly oxygen in its chemical behavior. Further research revealed instances of weight variation in other elements. It became clear to Soddy that some variations in the weight of nuclei were possible but that such variant atoms still retained the main properties of the original element as long as the electrical charge was correct. He called such overweight atoms *isotopes.* It was discovered later that some isotopes could be slightly underweight as well as overweight.

Atomic Structure

Rutherford returned to England from Canada and joined the faculty at Manchester University in 1907. There, he set out to measure the effect of alpha particles on still other materials. He had one of his students, Ernest Marsden, put a sample of uranium in a lead container that could be completely closed except for a narrow slit in one end. Rutherford expected that a steady stream of the alpha particles would emerge from the slit.

Marsden mounted a sheet of gold foil in front of the slit. The first test determined the number of particles that were stopped by the gold foil compared to the number that passed through it. A screen made with a coating of a phosphorous compound was placed behind the gold foil. A small spark occurred whenever the screen was struck by an alpha particle. Marsden's job was to count the sparks in a fixed time interval, first when the gold foil was present and then when it was removed. Almost all of the particles came through the gold foil, but the number of sparks was slightly less when the foil was present.

The next step was to determine the extent to which the alpha particles were bent from a perfectly straight path by passing

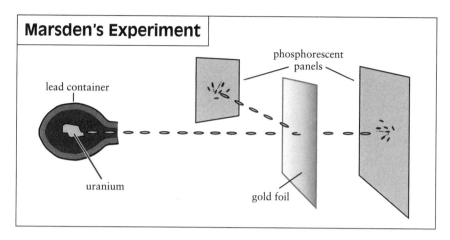

Marsden's Experiment

phosphorescent
panels

lead container

uranium

gold foil

Various outcomes from the irradiation of gold foil by alpha particles.
Many particles pass straight through the foil. Some are displaced slightly.
A very few recoil back toward the source.

through the foil. The idea was that if an alpha particle passed near enough to the nucleus of an atom of gold, it would have its path slightly bent. When the measurements were made, it was found that a few of the particles were indeed displaced.

Just to round out the sequence of observations, Marsden moved the screen to a position in front of the gold foil. The purpose was to see if any of the alpha particles were reflected back from the shiny gold foil. Rutherford and Marsden were very surprised to find that some particles were indeed bouncing back toward the source.

In sum, most of the particles went straight through the foil; a few of those that went through were deflected; and a very few bounced back from the foil toward the source. For Rutherford, the particles that bounced back were a problem. Based on the theoretical ideas that were dominant at that time, no such bounce-backs should occur—none at all.

Rutherford pondered the problem for one year. It then came to him that each atom of gold must have a core of very dense material but that this core was surrounded by empty or near-ly empty space. This empty space existed between the core and the electrons that balanced the core's positive electrical charge. This meant that even a solid material such as gold was really mostly empty space. The space between atoms is many thousands of times larger than the solid cores of such atoms. The empty space permitted almost all of the particles to go through the foil with no change in their path. A few particles came near enough to a nuclear core to be slightly deflected from their straight path. An even smaller fraction of the particles by chance struck a core head-on and were reflected back the way they had come.

Rutherford now conceived of the atomic structure as being similar to a solar system. The nucleus was heavy and dense and carried a positive charge. Its central location made it analogous to the Sun. Around this nucleus, at a great distance compared to the size of the nucleus, circled electrons in numbers that would balance the electrical charge of the nucleus. These electrons were seen to be analogous to the planets. This was an appealing image to many physicists; however, there were still problems. For example, no one could explain how the electrons maintained their orbital positions against the attraction of the positive charge of the nucleus. Also, atoms could emit light under certain conditions. This process was generally assigned to the orbiting electrons. But giving off light meant that they were also emitting energy. If that was true, they should lose velocity in their orbits and slowly but surely spiral down into the grasp of the nucleus.

The Bohr Atom

One of Rutherford's advanced students, Niels Bohr from Denmark, suggested that electrons are locked into certain orbits but that a shift from one orbital state to another can take place in an instant. Such orbital shifts could happen when light waves hit the atom. Some of the energy from the light could be absorbed by the electron, which would then shift into a higher orbit. If, for any reason, an electron were to descend from a high orbit to a lower orbit, light would be given off by the atom. An example would be the light from a firefly, which is the result of millions of electrons shifting into lower orbits and giving up energy. This effect is very different from anything that happens in a solar system.

Rutherford's solar system analogy also failed in another respect: the scale of distances. If the nucleus were the size of a basketball, the closest electron would be about 19 miles (about 30 km) away. In other words, if the nucleus were the size of the Sun, the planetlike electrons would be far out in the voids of space.

Likewise, the orbits of the electrons are not in a single plane as are the planets. Electron orbits can be at any angle to one another. Finally, electrons are not really solid objects like planets. In fact, they have no material counterpart in normal experience. Physicists try to convey their features by talking about fuzzy smears or cloudlike constructions, but these analogies are also misleading because electrons can sometimes act as if they are solid particles and sometimes as if they are waves. Perhaps the best way to describe an electron is that it is similar to a packet of energy with indistinct boundaries because of vibration.

The atom as conceived by Bohr consisted of two units: electrons in orbits around a core composed of protons. In ordinary atoms, the number of electrons was always equal to the number of protons. So, for example, according to the Bohr model, the lithium atom, which is next in mass after helium, was composed of three protons and three electrons. Nevertheless, the Bohr model left a serious mystery unexplained. With only three electrons and three protons, why did lithium weigh over seven times as much as a hydrogen atom? Clearly, more research was needed to solve this problem.

3

Progress Toward Nuclear Fission

The physical sciences, particularly nuclear studies, are characterized as depending on three distinct lines of work to achieve progress. The first line of work is observation and the collection of data from the conduct of what are called empirical experiments. The second line of work is the construction of theories, the propositions that explain what is observed and predict what will be observed under new or changed conditions. The third line of work is the development of instruments, to enhance the ability to observe or manipulate conditions so that the theories can be tested.

Generally, the three lines of work are pursued in parallel with bursts of activity in one line and then another. There was a burst of theorizing between 1900 and 1910 characterized by Albert Einstein's theory of relativity. The key feature of this theory for atomic scientists was the idea of the *photon*. According to Einstein, the photon was the unit of light energy that existed both as a particle and as a wave. This duality of form was the main barrier to wide acceptance and understanding of Einstein's work. Many people including many physicists resisted the idea that any object could be both a little particle and a wave of energy at the same time.

While Einstein's contribution to the understanding of the material universe was very important, the total period from around 1900 to 1920 was mainly devoted to empirical experimentation in the mode of Joseph John Thomson and Ernest Rutherford. During the 1920s, however, after two decades of intense observations, the emphasis truly shifted to theory.

Developing Theories

The principal theoretician during this stage was a German physicist named Werner Heisenberg. His theory was called quantum mechanics. The central idea contained in this theory is that the universe operates according to the rules of statistics or chance. This idea helped to explain how and why certain elements such as radium could go through radioactive decay by losing part of their nuclei in the form of groups of protons and neutral particles. Another prominent proposition from the theory was what is called the uncertainty principle. This principle recognizes that the act of observing influences that which is being observed—it changes it slightly. Basically, this idea simply meant that there were limits to what scientists could be absolutely sure about.

While theory dominated the decade of the 1920s, some

Erwin Schroedinger, an Austrian physicist, contributed greatly to the development of nuclear theory but as a pacifist did not participate in weapons research. (Courtesy of the CERN Historical Archives)

important observational research was also under way. Specifically, Victor Hess in Germany and Carl Anderson in the United States demonstrated the existence of very strong radiation that seemed to come from outer space. This radiation was given the name *cosmic rays*. Robert Millikan at the California Institute of Technology proved that the rays were composed of a variety of energetic particles that did not originate in the upper atmosphere of the Earth. Also, Anderson was able to prove that some of the cosmic rays were composed of *positrons*. These particles are similar to electrons in form and weight but carry a positive electrical charge rather than a negative charge. They are never incorporated into natural atoms, but their existence was a clue to the fact that there were probably other particles in addition to the electrons and protons that had been identified up to this time.

Smashing Atoms

In the early 1930s, the focus shifted again—first to instrumentation and then back to observation. The shift to instrumentation was prompted in part by calculations made by George Gamow in 1928 while working in Niels Bohr's laboratory in Denmark. Using Heisenberg's ideas, he determined the exact amount of energy required to drive an alpha particle from the nucleus of an atom. Gamow passed the information on to John Cockcroft and Ernest Walton, who were working with Rutherford at Cambridge University at the time. Rutherford encouraged Cockcroft and Walton to build a machine that could propel, or accelerate, protons up to the energy level specified by Gamow. In the spring of 1932, this primitive linear accelerator was completed, and experimentation could begin using protons that moved at energy levels equal to 700,000 electron volts. Success was immediate. The protons were fired into a sample of lithium, and some of the lithium atoms promptly broke apart, spewing alpha particles onto a radiation detector. The world's first atom smasher worked as predicted.

Meanwhile, studies using natural radiation were continuing in France. There in Paris, Marie and Pierre Curie's daughter, Irène Joliot-Curie, and son-in-law, Frédéric Joliot-Curie, carried on the tradition of research at the institute that the couple had founded, the Curie Institute of Radium. They were bombarding the hydrogen atoms in paraffin wax with particles from a high-powered mix of radium and beryllium. The radiation going into the paraffin was unusual in that it carried no electrical charge. It was strong enough, however, to dislodge the protons from the hydrogen atoms. Calculations done by a physicist named James Chadwick, who was working with Rutherford, showed that the radiation coming from the radium-beryllium mix had to have as much mass as the protons that were being dislodged. In this rather roundabout way the elusive *neutron* was finally uncovered. Prior to this discovery, the extra mass in the nucleus of atoms heavier than hydrogen could not be clearly explained. Now it was clear that the mass came from a distinctive particle: the neutron.

Part way around the world in California, Ernest Lawrence was perfecting the first accelerator that moved particles at progressively higher energy levels around a circular track. Lawrence called this machine a cyclotron. The cyclotron could be used to spawn neutrons and soon would allow scientists to see the full effects of the bombardment of heavy nuclei with such particles.

Lawrence was one of the few physicists after Millikan and Anderson to do research in the United States that was on a par with the work being done in Europe. Lawrence began attracting promising graduate students to his program at the University of California at Berkeley. In combination with the research in progress at the California Institute of Technology, the state of California was becoming an exciting place where advances were being made in the practical applications of particle physics. In particular, Lawrence's work led to the production of materials such as radioactive sodium and radioactive iodine, which were found to be useful in the medical treatment of certain cancers and other diseases.

Neutrons in Action

Once the neutron was identified, it became clear that the neutron was the source of the extra weight in the atoms larger than hydrogen. Scientists could now state that in such atoms there had to be at least one neutron in the nucleus for every proton. Most physicists came to believe that the neutron carried the force that held the otherwise mutually repellent protons closely together in the atom's core. As the number of protons in the nucleus increased beyond about 15, a surplus of neutrons was needed to accomplish the binding function. For example, lead has 82 protons but needs a total of 125 neutrons to hold the atom together. Consequently, the atomic weight of lead can be calculated by adding 82 and 125 to get 207.

The neutron source used by the Joliot-Curies also was able to generate radioactivity in elements such as aluminum. An unexpected result of these studies was the finding that the artificial radioactivity induced in aluminum is in the form of positron radiation identical to the cosmic-ray particles discovered by Anderson in the United States.

ENRICO FERMI'S CONTRIBUTIONS

Generally speaking, Italian scientists had not participated in the cascade of discoveries in nuclear science from the 1890s to the 1930s. In the golden age from 1900 to 1930, most of the finds were made in England, France, or Germany with a few key contributions from the United States. Enrico Fermi would restore the balance.

Born in Rome in 1901, Fermi was educated in Italy's public school system and was a top student and vigorous athlete as a schoolboy. Little formal instruction in physical science was available in the Italian schools, and Fermi was essentially self-taught in classical physics until he entered graduate school at the University of Pisa. He received his doctorate there at the young age of 21 and then did two years of postdoctoral work with Max Born at Born's institute in Göttingen, Germany. In the fall of 1924, Fermi returned to Italy and began his teaching career at the University of Florence.

His initial research work was mainly theoretical. It was of such high quality that he was invited to attend meetings of the top European physicists during the mid- to late 1920s. At one such meeting, in response to a suggestion by Wolfgang Pauli, he identified the properties of a particle that he termed a *neutrino*. The existence of such a particle was demanded by the current theory that required that all the properties of an atomic nucleus balance out. If a neutron consisted of only a proton that had swallowed an electron, the balance did not work out. Another very small electrically neutral particle was needed to reach the proper balance of forces. The actual existence of such a particle was later confirmed by the same sort of cosmic-ray research that had detected the positron.

Having so quickly established an international reputation, Fermi was invited to Rome, where he was instrumental in establishing the first school of modern physics at the city's university. There, in 1928, he married Laura Capon, the daughter of an admiral of the Italian navy.

After more work on mathematical theory, Fermi became intrigued with the concept of the neutron as laid out by the Joliot-Curies and Chadwick. He quickly saw that the neutron would be an ideal particle to use in the exploration of atomic nuclei. The neutron would generate less resistance to penetration because of its neutral electrical charge; simultaneously it would carry sufficient mass to move other nuclear particles when it collided with them.

In 1932, Fermi began to assemble a crude laboratory. He had to construct his own Geiger counter, a small device that registers the passage of charged particles. Such devices were not available for sale in Rome at that time. For his primary source of radiant energy, he was forced to borrow a gram of radium from Rome's public health office. With a mixture of beryllium and radium such as used by the Joliot-Curies, he was able to get a neutron flux: The alpha particles from the radium pushed neutrons out of the beryllium. With the output of neutrons, he could bombard other materials. He began a systematic examination of the effects of bombardment on as many elements as he could obtain in reasonably pure form.

Fermi's method was to start irradiating the lightest atoms and move progressively up the weight scale. Lithium showed no effect from bombardment. Boron showed no effect, nor did carbon, nitrogen, or oxygen. However, when fluorine was bombarded by neutrons, it became radioactive and began to spew out alpha particles.

Several other baffling effects were noted at certain stages in Fermi's series. One was the effect that came from slowing down the neutron. Fermi first noted that when the material to be irradiated with neutrons sat on a wooden table, the induced radioactivity was much stronger than when the material sat on a marble tabletop. This led Fermi to place barriers of various materials between the source of the rays and the material being irradiated. Soon he could show that when the barriers contained relatively light atoms, such as hydrogen, a strong magnification effect was generated. He speculated that the light nuclei of hydrogen had a braking effect on the neutron particles streaming by. When they were slowed, they had a greater chance of hitting the nucleus of one of the target atoms.

Another prospect occurred to Fermi when the team began to irradiate the heaviest atoms—including those that were already radioactive, such as uranium, the heaviest. Fermi made an early guess that totally new elements could be formed by neutron irradiation; atoms heavier than uranium might come into existence by absorbing either alpha particles or neutrons or both.

The most important finding, however, was that when heavy atoms such as uranium were irradiated with neutrons, more neutrons arose from the collisions than went into the collisions. In other words there was a multiplier effect. Along with the increase in the actual number of neutrons, there was a release of energy. The materials under neutron bombardment and those nearby became hot. The thought arose in Fermi's mind that if some neutrons generated more neutrons, something like a chain reaction might be produced. A significant side effect of such a chain reaction would be the release of a large quantity of energy.

Beyond Uranium

For most physicists, the finding that most strongly invited further research was the hint that uranium or the other very heavy metals were capable of absorbing protons or alpha particles that had been knocked loose from other atoms by the neutron bombardment. Among these physicists, one of the most fascinated was Lise Meitner, a professor and department head at the Kaiser Wilhelm Institute in Berlin, Germany.

From time to time, Meitner had teamed with Otto Hahn, a senior chemist who also headed a department at the institute. The pair had discovered the heavy element protactinium in 1918. This discovery had come about in the course of alpha particle irradiation of other elements. Their success set the stage for their excitement about Fermi's findings. If Fermi was correct, Meitner and Hahn might be able to find other new elements or actually create new elements that would be heavier than uranium.

Meitner took the lead in suggesting a renewal of their collaboration to pursue this new line of research. By the end of 1934, preliminary results suggested that Fermi's ideas about the production of new elements were correct. There were problems, however, in isolating the tiny amounts of each element from the jumble that remained in the target material after it was irradiated with the neutrons.

LISE MEITNER

Meitner was born into a large, upper-middle-class Viennese family in 1878. She was encouraged by her parents to pursue her intellectual interests despite a social background that did not support such activities for women. Fortunately, the University of Vienna saw fit to admit women in 1900, and Meitner was able to complete her doctorate there by 1904. After some preliminary research on radioactivity, she moved in 1907 to Berlin, Germany, where she began her intermittent collaboration with Otto Hahn.

In 1934, when she and Hahn started their followup research of Fermi's findings, Germany was in turmoil due to economic inflation. The government under the newly elected chancellor Adolf Hitler was beginning to punish anyone who disagreed with his policies. By that time, Meitner was already a renowned physicist. Her prominence in the field and her Austrian citizenship inhibited the German officials under Hitler from dismissing her from her position because she was Jewish. She was able to retain her position even when other Jewish professors were being forced out.

She made the best use of her time by continuing to examine the result of sending neutrons into a uranium target. Because the mix of end products from the neutron bombardment of uranium continued to be puzzling, Meitner and Hahn decided to add a young analytical chemist, Fritz Strassmann, to the team.

The confusion about the identity of the end products was based on two strong but mistaken assumptions. First, all the previous research suggested that nuclear reactions produced only small changes in the target atoms. Second, they expected that any elements heavier than uranium that might be produced would have chemical reactions similar to those of the so-called transition elements such as iridium and platinum. Indeed, Hahn and Strassmann were observing

Lise Meitner demonstrated in laboratory experiments how neutrons could split a uranium atom. (Courtesy of the CERN Historical Archives)

such chemical reactions in the residue of the uranium bombardments. All in all, the evidence allowed for several conjectures about the details of the process. However, Meitner saw flaws in all the new ideas.

In the early spring of 1938, the German army, in a move directed by Hitler, moved across the undefended border of Austria. Austria was subsequently annexed to Germany, and all Austrians immediately became German citizens. Through that summer and into the autumn months, a campaign against all German citizens of Jewish descent was initiated by the authorities, and many Jews were arrested and removed to concentration camps. Meitner's safety was no longer assured. She was forced to flee to Denmark and from there to seek haven in Sweden. Soon, World War II broke out.

In the meantime, Hahn and Strassmann continued to analyze the materials produced by the uranium bombardment. At the same time, the Joliot-Curies in Paris were finding strange results from some parallel experiments. They seemed to be getting a variant of radium as a collision product. The radium variant was extracted along with some barium, which was considered to be a contamination of the materials used in the study. Hahn and Strassman were informed of this result, and when they looked for barium in their residue, they also found some.

By secret contacts and by disguised mail, Meitner kept urging Hahn and Strassmann to redo the radium analysis. When they did, it became certain that the product was not radium but indeed barium. Barium weighed only a little more than half as much as uranium. This meant that the uranium atom had split into two large pieces. While it is possible to make a uranium atom—and other atoms as well—gain weight by irradiation with neutrons or other atomic nuclei, no one thought that one could split an atom in two. Now scientists saw that such *fission* was not only possible but that it might be brought under human control.

Once the minds of the scientists had fully grasped the meaning of this discovery, they soon found that the uranium atom not only split but that the products of the split tended to decay into still other elements. At least eight medium weight elements can be produced. It was no wonder that the chemistry had been confused.

Because of World War II, primarily between Germany and Japan on one side and Great Britain, the United States, and the Soviet Union on the other, as well as the internal German political situation, Meitner was excluded from the Nobel Prize awarded to Hahn in 1944 for splitting the uranium atom. She remained in Sweden as a teacher and retired to Cambridge, England, in 1960. She died there in 1968 near the end of her 89th year.

4

Nuclear Energies

Because of her relative isolation in Sweden, Lise Meitner reached out to colleagues in England during the late 1930s. Among this group of scientists was Meitner's nephew Otto Frisch. These two physicists wrote the first comprehensive explanation of nuclear fission. Later, in 1940, Frisch and some colleagues calculated the potential energy that could be generated from such fission. This analysis demonstrated that powerful weapons might be developed from uranium.

Indeed, for some time, scientists had considered the likelihood that such a weapon was possible. In 1933, at a meeting of the British Association for the Advancement of Science, Ernest Rutherford had discussed the prospect of extracting massive amounts of energy from nuclear fission. He was discouraged, however, by the results of his own studies: His research seemed to indicate that a disproportionate amount of energy was needed to trigger the required reactions.

Leo Szilard, a Hungarian scientist who had escaped from Germany to England, read a report of Rutherford's pessimistic talk with great interest. Soon, Szilard became convinced that Rutherford was wrong and that a more economical, spontaneous chain reaction could be established to trigger reactions. He was aware that the unstable uranium atoms spontaneously released alpha particles. Szilard believed that each uranium atom would release more than one particle when bombarded with neutrons. If this assumption was correct, then the resultant energy would allow a more economically feasible chain reaction and might produce the fission needed to make an atomic weapon. Szilard's analytical research proved this theory to be correct. His detailed analysis of the uranium chain reaction led to the award of a British patent in 1934, but he soon became worried that his discovery might be picked up by the Germans. To keep his breakthrough from becoming public, he assigned the patent to the British navy. In addition, he did not publish any reports in the scientific literature. His findings were not known to other scientists until six years had passed.

Early Weapons Studies

By the mid-1930s, physicists knew that there are two factors required for a controllable chain reaction. One is the "enrichment" of the mass of uranium used in the reaction. In natural uranium, the more-active isotope, uranium 235, makes up only about 1 percent of the mass, and the less-active uranium 238 makes up the remaining 99 percent. Years before, Niels Bohr had calculated that the chain reaction would be easier if the proportion of uranium 235 were slightly increased to 4 percent or 5 percent. This increase is called "enrichment."

The second factor is control of the velocity of the neutrons released in the chain reaction. In 1934, Enrico Fermi established that an unstable uranium atom released two or three particles when it was struck by a slowed neutron. Scientists discovered that the speed of the incoming neutron can be slowed by placing a barrier of heavy water or graphite in its path. To achieve the best results, the rate of the incoming neutron must be equal to the rate of the rhythmic vibrations within the uranium nucleus. The nuclei of all atoms—excepting hydrogen atoms, which have no neutrons—vibrate at a distinctive rate.

In 1939, this knowledge and the release of new information on atomic fission renewed interest in the possibility of weapons development. All physicists were in agreement that successful fission could be the result of a controllable chain reaction. Even before the fission studies were published, chain reactions were being investigated at several sites. At first, these inquiries had ended in failure; however, in the spring of 1939, the Joliot-Curie team in Paris demonstrated a method that could double or triple the neutrons released by a chain reaction.

By 1939, Fermi and Szilard were working together on a project at Columbia University in New York City. That same year, positive results were obtained from their work and the similar project headed by the Joliot-Curie team. Szilard was worried about the prospect of weapons development and wanted to keep the New York findings secret. He asked Joliot-Curie to suppress the Paris findings as well. However, the tradition of free information exchange in science was too strong: The French scientists published their results. Soon, the New Yorkers announced their discovery, as well.

Conditions were now ready for weapons development to begin. The physics of both the chain reaction and the nuclear fission reaction had been revealed by scientists in Paris and New York. Scientists in other countries such as Japan and the Soviet Union saw the possibility of future weapons and began their own research programs.

The German Effort

Because of their war effort, the Germans were also ready to activate research projects to develop new weapons. In spring 1939, two agencies of the German government, the Ministry of Education and the War Ministry, were alerted to the prospect of atomic weapons. The Ministry of Education became involved because of the university affiliations of the participating scientists. A few months later, in the early days of World War II, officials of the German war ministry hosted a meeting of the best German physicists and nuclear chemists. The group of scientists included Werner Heisenberg, Hans Geiger, and Otto Hahn. They quickly prepared an overall strategic plan for the military application of nuclear fission. The Kaiser Wilhelm Institute in Berlin was designated as the center for fission research.

At that time, a Dutch scientist, Peter Debye, was the director of the institute. German military officials did not want a non-German to have administrative responsibilities for the research on secret weapons, so Debye was asked to resign. The Dutchman soon immigrated to the United States and helped alert the Americans to German research on atomic weapons.

The Germans, meanwhile, selected Kurt Diebner to replace Debye. Diebner was a physicist of modest talents but with strong Nazi beliefs. Although Diebner was the director, the brilliant Heisenberg was by far the most influential scientist on the project. Heisenberg's great abilities allowed him to dominate the planning and decision-making for the entire effort.

Heisenberg laid out two major goals. As Niels Bohr had suggested as a necessary step, Heisenberg sought to increase the proportion of the lighter and more active uranium 235 from about 1 percent found in natural uranium to about 5 percent in enriched uranium. This would decrease the heavier and less active uranium 238 from 99 percent to about 95 percent and allow better conditions for a sustained and controlled chain reaction. A method called thermal diffusion was chosen to achieve the goal. In this technique, gaseous uranium is introduced at the bottom of an array of vertical pipes. A heated metal rod stands in the center of each pipe while the outer walls of the pipe are kept cooled. When the uranium gas is diffused into the pipes, the lighter atoms (uranium 235) are attracted to the heated rod in the center and move upward. The heavier atoms (uranium 238) are attracted to the colder outer walls of the pipe and stay down. The more valuable uranium 235 can be collected at the top of the pipe array.

Under the best conditions, this separation process was very slow and imprecise. The problem was compounded because the most convenient gaseous form of uranium is the highly corrosive uranium tetrafluoride (UF_4). Because uranium tetrafluoride is especially corrosive at high temperatures, the vertical pipes were always being damaged.

Heisenberg simultaneously sought new methods to achieve a sustained chain reaction. He knew that the natural velocity of the neutrons can be slowed by certain materials. The possible materials included ordinary water, paraffin wax, frozen carbon dioxide (dry ice), graphite (pencil lead), and heavy water (D_2O). Ordinary water not only slows neutrons but also absorbs many of them, so it was not suitable. Such absorption tends to shut down the reaction. Wax and dry ice can be used in experiments but are vaporized by the intense heat of a large-scale chain reaction. Graphite is the best material because it can be made to conform to the structures used for the reaction, but the Germans had serious difficulties in obtaining graphite of sufficient purity. Heavy water, therefore, became the material of choice. The Germans set out to obtain sufficient quantities.

In January 1940, the Germans sent a trade delegation to Norway. The Norwegians had a large fertilizer factory in Rjukan, and a by-product of fertilizer production is heavy water. The German delegation offered to buy all the available stocks of heavy water. Although they could not explain their interest, the Germans also tried to persuade the Norwegians to increase fertilizer production by a factor of 10.

When French government officials learned of the German attempt to buy a large amount of heavy water, they deduced that the Germans were trying to build a nuclear reactor. The French immediately sent a special agent to Norway. The agent happened to be a part owner of the fertilizer plant and persuaded the other owners to allocate the heavy water to the French rather than the Germans.

In spring 1940, the Germans invaded France and quickly reached Paris. However, French scientists had been able to remove the heavy water and place it aboard an English ship. The French physicists and the heavy water were soon transported to England and escaped the German invaders.

That summer, the Germans invaded Norway and Denmark. They easily gained control of the Norwegian production of heavy water. Although a British commando raid failed to destroy the fertilizer plant, Norwegian partisans eventually disrupted the production. This loss further impaired the ineffective German nuclear effort.

At the outbreak of World War II, Germany had more nuclear scientists than any other country. In spite of this, the German effort to produce atomic weapons was a serious failure. Several reasons may have contributed to this condition.

As the war progressed, elements of the German bureaucracy began to compete against one another. This competition upset the sharp concentration needed to reach a successful conclusion to their weapons project. Atomic research also suffered from mistakes made by scientists and military leaders. An important example was their incorrect choice of thermal diffusion as a method to enrich uranium. Indeed, some historians conclude that Heisenberg carefully undermined the German war effort by overestimating the amount of enriched uranium needed to build a nuclear weapon. Near the end of the war, the Germans gave the nuclear weapons project a low priority. Materials and labor for other last-minute weapons such as ballistic missiles and jet aircraft were believed by Hitler to be far more important to their war effort.

Heisenberg and a handful of scientists and technicians were captured by the American army in Bavaria and taken to England in the spring of 1945. The war in Europe was over; however, the war between the United States and its allies and Japan continued. While Heisenberg was in custody, the Americans dropped two nuclear bombs in Japan. He was astonished to hear that the Americans had succeeded in an undertaking that the Germans had been unable to complete.

The British Effort

When France fell and the French physicists escaped to England with their supply of heavy water, the British authorities reactivated their weapons program. They asked Frisch and other refugees to prepare a planning study for such a project. The study focused on the design of a bomb rather than issues such as the construction of a reactor with a self-sustaining chain reaction. The British knew that Fermi was working toward that goal in the United States and was in a better position to succeed than the English scientists were.

In April 1940, a British management committee established four research and development teams. The teams were located at the universities of Oxford, Cambridge, Liverpool, and Birmingham. The large British company Imperial Chemical

British Uranium Bomb

3,000 ft./sec.   3,000 ft./sec.

5 kg   10 kg
(critical mass
required for fission)   5 kg

U-235   ordinary explosive

The British design for a uranium bomb called for explosive charges at each end of a tube to drive shaped pieces of uranium 235 together in the middle. The two pieces were to form a critical mass that would detonate in a violent fission reaction.

Industries, Ltd., was also brought into the project. The company was chosen to build and operate the facilities for the separation and refinement of uranium 235 into metallic form.

At the end of 18 months, the British concluded that a bomb could be constructed. They were confident that only about 22 pounds (10 kg) of purified uranium was needed for the project. Although this bomb was never built, a slightly modified version of the British design was adopted by the Americans and used for the bomb dropped on Hiroshima.

By early 1942, the U.S. Army was funding a large and expensive effort toward bomb production. By now, the cost of waging war had left the British military with limited resources. The two countries decided to combine their research programs and a uranium enrichment facility was built in Canada. The facility was available to British and American scientists and safe from the bombs of the German air force.

Other Countries in the Race

Little has come to light about early nuclear projects conducted in other countries. Reports from the late 1930s and early 1940s seem to show that both the Soviet Union and Japan were involved in some level of research. Apparently, the Soviet effort was extensive, and routine progress was made during World War II. On the other hand, the Japanese effort was limited and given a low priority. At the time, Japan had few nuclear scientists. These Japanese physicists were influenced by the German idea that a nuclear bomb could not be produced without a massive expenditure of funds. The Japanese could not afford to make such a commitment. The Allies would take first place in the race to develop nuclear weapons.

5
The Atomic Bomb

By summer 1939, the first wave of central European scientists had immigrated to the United States. Enrico Fermi was at Columbia University in New York City; the influential theoretician Hans Bethe was at Cornell University in Ithaca, New York; George Gamow was at George Washington University in Washington, D.C.; and Albert Einstein was at Princeton University in New Jersey.

Building Resources

Historians estimate that approximately 20 to 25 top-notch, American-born atomic scientists lived in the United States in 1939. Between 1933 and 1939, about the same number immigrated to the United States from central Europe. Therefore, the number of high-level nuclear physicists working in America had doubled in that six-year span.

Among the émigrés were the Hungarians Leo Szilard, Eugene Paul Wigner, and Edward Teller, who would later play a crucial role in developing the hydrogen bomb. Szilard, who had fled from Nazi Germany, was troubled that the Germans might produce a nuclear weapon. He was more alarmed after the German Otto Hahn achieved uranium fission. When the Joliot-Curie team in Paris and his own team in the United States each developed a method to multiply the original number of neutrons obtained by a chain reaction, Szilard became distraught. He requested that the Joliot-Curies and others working on nuclear research withhold the publication of their results. He believed that such self-censorship would help prevent German scientists from making rapid advances in their design of atomic weapons. However, Szilard's scheme was not workable because he could not enforce a ban on publications.

Szilard next presented a plan for nuclear weapons to be developed in the United States. He knew that funding was essential but—like many scientists of that era—regarded government funding as overly restrictive. Many believed that government officials would impose too many bureaucratic constraints on the research. However, the possibility of private funding seemed bleak. Szilard and his friends were unacquainted with philanthropic foundations in the United States and were worried that their foreign origins would cause prospective donors to hesitate. So, against their better judgment, they sought the endorsement of the United States government. They hoped that a letter of governmental endorsement would encourage private donors.

Szilard, Wigner, and Teller decided that their plan would gain credibility with the backing of a great physicist such as Einstein. Since the three men had known Einstein for many years, they asked him to sign a letter that they had written to Franklin Roosevelt, president of the United States. The letter was hand-carried to the president by his longtime friend Alexander Sachs. Sachs was an economist interested in the science of physics and acquainted with Wigner.

As expected, Roosevelt was impressed by both the contents and the signer of the message. The president strongly endorsed the idea of developing an atomic bomb but misunderstood the objective of the letter. Rather than encouraging the participation of private philanthropy, he appointed a special government committee and chose a senior government scientist to

Albert Einstein in conversation with Wolfgang Pauli at a time before Einstein moved permanently to the United States. (Courtesy of the Photographic Service of the Library of Congress)

head the group. Roosevelt selected Lyman Briggs, the director of the Bureau of Standards, for this position. The newly formed Uranium Committee called in consultants who had current knowledge of all the nuclear research efforts. By the time the German army invaded Poland in September 1939, the committee had reported that a nuclear weapon was possible.

Wartime Research

After the outbreak of World War II in 1939, officials of the U.S. government created a more focused planning group. Szilard was asked to attend the panel's conferences. He discussed the research that he and Fermi were conducting at Columbia University. He also shared with the panel his belief that atomic fission might be used to power naval warships. An admiral on the panel became interested in this concept and asked Szilard to estimate the funding needed for further studies. Szilard asked for and received $6,000 but a few months later sought an additional $50,000. Eventually, the funds were awarded to him. At that time, $50,000 was a very large amount of money.

In spite of some government funding for nuclear research, few advances were made in university research or weapons development programs. A second letter from Einstein, in early 1942, directed to the Uranium Committee, was intended to reawaken the effort. In 1942, the Allies in Europe and Africa were suffering from military setbacks and Einstein's letter was carefully considered; in fact, the letter led to the creation of the National Defense Research Committee (NDRC). President Roosevelt assigned the responsibility for monitoring the nuclear weapons program to this new agency. Roosevelt selected Vannevar Bush, then head of the Carnegie Institute, as director of the organization. Bush was a well-connected, experienced leader, who had the respect of the scientific, engineering, and industrial communities.

In early 1941, a discovery by the American chemist Edwin McMillan advanced the prospect of nuclear weapons. While using the cyclotron at the Berkeley campus of the University of California,

Glenn Seaborg was the first person to produce the synthetic element plutonium by the bombardment of uranium with protons in a cyclotron. (Courtesy of the Lawrence Berkeley National Laboratory)

McMillan created neptunium, element 93, from the irradiation of uranium with neutrons. At last, Fermi was proven correct in his belief that such irradiation could produce heavier elements than uranium. McMillan demonstrated that some uranium atoms become heavier elements when their nuclei absorb alpha particles released from other uranium atoms.

Quickly, followup research was begun at the university by scientists such as the American chemist Glenn Seaborg, who was also using the Lawrence cyclotron. In a few weeks, the physicists created the relatively stable plutonium, element 94. A few days later, Italian-born Emilio Segrè demonstrated that plutonium could be used as a fuel in an atomic reactor. Seaborg and Segrè realized that plutonium might be vastly superior to uranium as an explosive material. Although plutonium was relatively difficult to produce, it was easy to purify and might give a higher energy yield than uranium.

On June 15, 1941, President Roosevelt again increased the government's efforts to utilize science and technology to support national security. He initiated the Office of Scientific Research and Development (OSRD). Bush took over as its head. This organization was made a part of the Office of Emergency Management, which reported directly to the president. Bush's authority was strengthened by this change, and the morale of the nuclear scientists greatly improved. They had been worried that the government would act indecisively about the threat of a German atomic bomb.

The Pace Picks Up

In August 1941, an emissary from the British nuclear weapons group arrived in the United States. He brought the report that a bomb might be made with as little as 22 pounds (10 kg) of highly purified uranium 235. However, the report failed to interest Briggs, the civilian head of the original Uranium

Committee. In desperation, the British scientist went to the University of California at Berkeley and conferred with Ernest Lawrence, the cyclotron builder. Lawrence saw the need for immediate action. He escorted the emissary to James Conant, the scientist in charge of the uranium program in partnership with Bush at the NDRC. Conant was excited by the message and quickly told Bush of the startling communication. Bush was also impressed by the information; however, he realized that taking action would be costly and require an administrator familiar with large-scale production operations.

After careful consideration, Bush requested the army to supervise the design of atomic weapons and the production of enriched uranium and purified plutonium. Colonel Leslie Groves from the Army Corps of Engineers was appointed to oversee the operation. Groves had been deputy chief of construction of the Pentagon in Arlington, Virginia. At that time, the Pentagon was the largest office building in the world. Groves had gained prominence by finishing the job before the scheduled deadline and below the estimated cost.

LESLIE GROVES

Groves was born in Albany, New York, in 1896. His father was a Protestant minister, who become an army chaplain when Leslie was about four years old. Groves entered the U.S. Military Academy at West Point, New York, in 1914. Four years later, he graduated fourth in his class. Groves was too young to participate in the battles of World War I. However, as a career officer in the Corps of Engineers, he served at many different posts between the two world wars. He attained the rank of colonel because of his outstanding performance in building the Pentagon. Throughout his military career, Groves was widely regarded as a strict, serious, and hard-working leader. Although he did not seek the affection of subordinates, he gained their respect.

After learning of Groves's appointment, a few high government officials worried that the colonel would have difficulty working with scientists. The officials were concerned that the military value system would be incompatible with that of the academic community, but with few exceptions, the arrangement brought only mutual respect.

Groves was soon promoted to the rank of brigadier general. On September 17, 1942—eight months after the United States had entered the war—he was in charge of the entire atomic bomb project. (The United States had quickly entered World War II on December 8, 1941, a day after Nazi Germany's ally Japan bombed an American military base at Pearl Harbor, Hawaii, in a devastating surprise attack.) Meanwhile, Groves ordered the construction of massive facilities to refine uranium and plutonium.

Bush had laid out the guidelines for the vast atomic weapons program and arranged the necessary political backing. He was confident that Groves would keep production under reasonable control but recognized that the research aspects of the program needed the attentions of a scientist. In May 1942, Bush named J. Robert Oppenheimer, an outstanding theoretical physicist from the University of California at Berkeley, to serve as research and development coordinator for all weapons production.

ROBERT OPPENHEIMER

Oppenheimer came from a wealthy family. His father owned a prosperous garment business in New York City, and his mother was a talented painter. Julius Robert was born in 1904. He never liked his first name and was called Bob or Robert until he entered graduate school. At this point, fellow students coined the nickname Oppy.

Oppenheimer graduated a year early from Harvard with an honors degree in chemistry. After a year of graduate work at

Robert Oppenheimer led the team of scientists and technicians who produced the first atomic bombs. (Courtesy of the CERN Historical Archives)

the Cavendish Laboratory at Cambridge University in England, he went on to study theory at Göttingen in Germany and finished his doctorate in 1927. Oppenheimer returned to the United States and accepted a faculty position shared between the University of California at Berkeley and the California Institute of Technology at Pasadena. At that time, both universities were major centers for nuclear research.

Oppenheimer was popular with his students and enjoyed his successful teaching career. He was reluctant to interrupt his pleasant life to accept a position for the scientific management of a weapons development program. Most historians believe that Hitler's rise to power motivated Oppenheimer's decision to take the job in 1942. Hitler was violently anti-Semitic and Oppenheimer was Jewish. Also, Oppenheimer was sympathetic toward the ideals of world communism. The U.S.S.R., at war with Nazi Germany, was a communist state. These beliefs probably contributed to his desire to ensure the defeat of Nazi Germany in the war.

The Chicago Organization

Soon after Oppenheimer's acceptance, Bush transferred Fermi and his team of scientists from Columbia University to the

Metallurgical Laboratory at the University of Chicago. This move consolidated various groups of scientists now involved in a single project. The team members, which included Fermi, Szilard, Wigner, and other physicists who joined a team that had been led by the physicist Samuel Allison, sought to develop a controlled chain reaction in a type of reactor called a pile.

The components used to build the pile were blocks of uranium metal, aluminum canisters of uranium oxide powder, and blocks of graphite. The graphite served to moderate the velocity of the neutrons produced by the uranium. At the center of the pile, the few blocks of pure uranium metal were stacked between blocks of graphite. The next layers consisted of aluminum containers of uranium oxide powder and blocks of graphite. The outer walls were made completely of graphite.

The completed pile was a large cube, about nine feet (just under 3 m) on a side. Recording instruments and controls were placed in channels cut into the otherwise solid structure. The main control was a cadmium foil-wrapped wooden arm almost seven feet (2 m) long. Cadmium rapidly absorbs neutrons and can suppress a chain reaction. Additional cadmium was mixed with water and kept ready as a safety precaution. During tests of the pile, technicians with buckets of the mixture stood on a platform above the pile. If signs of overheating occurred, they were to pour out the liquid and stop the reaction.

After many weeks of preliminary testing, the pile was ready for operation. During the morning and early afternoon of December 2, 1942, the control arm was slowly retracted from the center of the pile. At 3:25 P.M. the arm was completely withdrawn and a self-sustaining chain reaction was achieved. For the first time—just one week short of the first anniversary of the Japanese bombing of Pearl Harbor—scientists controlled the release of a large amount of nuclear energy and had proven the certainty of a self-sustained chain reaction.

The success of the Chicago project provided an alternative to the cyclotron for the production of elements heavier than uranium. The University of Chicago team had demonstrated that uranium was transmuted into plutonium during the chain reaction in the pile.

The Buildup

In order to disguise their true purpose, all funds for atomic research and nuclear weapon development were funneled through the Corps of Engineers. An uninteresting name, the Manhattan Engineer District, provided a cover for the project. (The project became better known as simply the Manhattan Project.)

The first objective of the secret project was to boost the production of enriched uranium. The goal was to increase the 1 percent proportion of uranium 235 found in natural uranium up to a level that would support spontaneous fission.

For safety and military security concerns, Groves and other government officials wanted uranium production facilities located at a distance from big cities and extensive metropolitan areas. In the early 1930s, the government had purchased large amounts of land in central Tennessee for the Tennessee Valley Project, under which dams were built to generate electricity for the rural Appalachian Mountains region. Surplus government land was available near the small town of Oak Ridge, Tennessee. At this site production facilities for the project were built far from any big city on low-cost land with plenty of available electric power. Groves supervised the construction of the enrichment plant and the facilities needed for a large work-force. Several companies were awarded contracts to build the plants and design the massive machines to separate the uranium isotopes. Eventually, the Union Carbide Corporation was designated to act as site manager. During the duration of the war, the facility at Oak Ridge served as one of Groves's main bases of operation.

Work on a plutonium production facility soon followed. The DuPont Chemical Company was contracted to provide the overall management. The plant was built on a vast plateau in western Washington State near the town of Hanford. This area was chosen because when plutonium is produced by the irradiation of uranium, water is required to cool the reactors. The Columbia River flows along the north side of the site and provides a plentiful supply of moving water. Groves was aware that the river water would retain some of the heat absorbed from the reactors. Fish biologists assured him that the warmer water would not harm the salmon that spawned in the upper reaches of the river.

This calutron prototype is being repaired. The device was designed to separate the isotope, uranium 235, from uranium stock. Many larger versions of the machine were installed at the Oak Ridge, Tennessee, site. (Courtesy of the National Archives and Records Administration)

Oppenheimer decided to centralize all scientific activities at a third location. He believed that the people involved in these undertakings would gain team spirit if they lived and worked at the same site. Although this large concentration of workers did not fit well with the need for secrecy, Oppenheimer persuaded Groves to house all the scientists and engineers in a single, remote place.

After looking at a number of places in the Southwest, Groves and Oppenheimer agreed that a site near Los Alamos, New Mexico, was nearly ideal. Indeed, some of the buildings needed for offices, laboratories, and residences already existed on the Los Alamos mesa. They were on the campus of the Ranch School for Boys, a high-priced educational facility for about 45 children. In 1942, the Secretary of the Army requested that the boys move out. The soldiers and scientists immediately moved in and began work on the atomic bomb design. (By this point, the war against Japan in the Pacific had become extremely destructive, adding even more urgency to the development of new weapons.)

Weapon Development and Assembly

Scientists were not confident that a plutonium bomb was possible until two years after the founding of the Los Alamos facility. By 1943, however, they were positive that a successful atomic weapon could be made with purified uranium. Scientists knew that a sphere-shaped "critical mass" of metallic uranium 235 (of about 22 pounds, or 10 kg) would ignite spontaneously. Critical mass was the amount of a radioactive element needed for an atomic explosion. The critical mass for metallic uranium 235 had been established by British mathematical analyses and verified by American computations. This weight and the spherical shape ensured that the spontaneous flow of neutrons from some of the uranium 235 atoms would cause other uranium atoms to split and violently release a wave of pure energy.

Although the production of a uranium bomb is complicated, the principle is fairly simple. In order to achieve the critical mass necessary for an atomic explosion, scientists must shape a piece of metallic uranium into two half-spheres (hemispheres). The two portions of uranium are then placed in a tube (like the barrel of a cannon) and forced together in a violent and rapid manner. British scientists had designed a device in which a hemisphere of metallic uranium was placed at each end of a tube. An explosive charge was secured behind each hemisphere. When the charges exploded, the segments of ura-

The Y-12 area at Oak Ridge, Tennessee, housed the industrial facilities for the separation of isotopes of uranium. (Courtesy of the U.S. Department of Energy)

nium were rapidly propelled into the center of the tube and formed a critical mass. The Americans improved the design by securing one of the uranium hemispheres at one end of the tube and firing the other into it. This modification required only one explosive charge and helped eliminate the possibility of a misfire. The American-designed uranium bomb was not field-tested before the successful bombing of Hiroshima in August 1945. This lack of testing is credited to the Americans' confidence in their bomb and their reluctance to employ the scarce metallic uranium 235 to build a bomb for testing purposes. Work went ahead on a uranium bomb to be used against the Japanese in the Pacific.

Meanwhile, plutonium, produced in reactors by the irradiation of the more plentiful uranium 238, was easier to obtain than uranium 235. However, the design of the plutonium

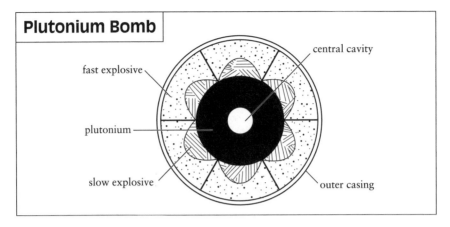

The plutonium bomb used chemical explosives to force the fissionable material into a compact sphere. Slow and fast explosives helped to ensure that all the plutonium moved at the same time and at the same speed.

bomb was far more complicated than that of the uranium weapon. While uranium is a rather brittle metal, plutonium is relatively soft and can be compressed. Laboratory studies indicated that a small amount (about seven pounds, or 3 kg) of plutonium would ignite if properly compressed into a critical mass. To achieve the critical mass, specially shaped charges of high explosive materials were placed behind wedges of plutonium in a large sphere-shaped container. When fired, the explosives drove the plutonium into the center of the container where it formed into a compressed mass. The walls of the container were made of a dense, reflective metal. During the explosion, some of the resultant neutrons escaped, but some were reflected back into the center of the reaction and generated additional neutrons and energy.

Since the more stable plutonium spontaneously releases fewer neutrons than uranium 235, the weapon had to include another radioactive element to serve as a "primer." (A primer is a material that accelerates any type of reaction.) In this case,

The bomb assembly shed was not an attractive building—but that helped to shroud its purposes in secrecy. (Courtesy of the U.S. Department of Energy)

the primer chosen to help speed the atomic reaction was the element polonium—discovered by Marie and Pierre Curie many years before. The weapon designers knew that polonium spontaneously releases a plentiful supply of neutrons needed for a successful reaction; therefore, a golf ball-size sphere of the substance was placed in the center of the plutonium mass.

In order to properly compress the critical mass of plutonium, the ideal shape, position, timing, and force of the explosive devices required extensive testing. Twenty dummy weapons (containing nonnuclear material) were used to determine the best of the possibilities.

Trinity

Preparations for the test of the plutonium bomb began in July 1944. The code name for the test was "Trinity," and scientists hoped to conduct the Trinity test in midsummer 1945. An ideal site was found within 220 miles (about 350 km) of Los Alamos at an Army Air Corps training area near Alamagordo, New Mexico. The nearest town was more than 27 miles (about 43 km) distant from "ground zero" (the explosion's center). A 20-mile (32-km) section of the desert was closed off, and construction of the test facilities began in autumn 1944. Many months of intense labor followed the completion of the arrangements.

A final full-fledged dress rehearsal was conducted on May 7, 1945, at Alamagordo. A dummy bomb containing conventional explosive devices but without the plutonium core was raised on a tower identical to that to be used in the actual test.

The outer casing of the plutonium bomb was code-named "Fat Man" for obvious reasons. (Courtesy of the U.S. National Archives and Records Administration)

The rehearsal went well. A few lapses in instrumentation and communications were remedied before the actual test.

The Alamagordo test site was undergoing final preparation for the actual plutonium bomb test when the uranium bomb arrived at the Tinian Island Air Base in the far Pacific. The B-29 bomber designated to carry the uranium bomb to Hiroshima in Japan had been refitted to carry its deadly weapon, but high military officials had decided that the uranium bomb should not be used until the basic concept had been verified by the test of the plutonium bomb.

Finally, the Alamagordo site was ready. The bomb itself was about six feet (almost 2 m) in diameter and weighed more than 6,000 pounds (about 3,000 kg). The detonation site was a tower about 100 feet (30 m) in height. Hundreds of

The Trinity Monument marks the spot where the first atomic bomb was detonated. (Courtesy of the U.S. National Archives and Records Administration)

instruments had been placed in the ground at various distances from the tower. Scientists needed to gain information about the heat and pressure of the blast as well as the effects of the radiation.

On the night before the test, a nervous group of project scientists, engineers, technicians, and government officials

The Enola Gay was the B-29 bomber that carried the uranium bomb to Hiroshima in August 1945. (Courtesy of the U.S. National Archives and Records Administration)

gathered at the site. An evening rainstorm added to their worries. Nevertheless, the successful detonation occurred at 5:30 A.M. on Monday, July 16, 1945. The historic event was witnessed by many distinguished scientists and government officials including Robert Oppenheimer and Leslie Groves. These two men had risked their honor and reputations on a successful test.

The test was more awe inspiring than anyone had expected. For many, including Oppenheimer, the event was similar to a religious experience. The initial burst of light was so intense that people who were 10 miles (16 km) away from the blast had to close their eyes and look away. Some lost their vision for a few minutes. Others were disoriented for a longer period by the intense flash of light. Even miles away, the noise of the explosion and the force of the wind were intense. The strength of the blast was calculated to be equal to 17,000 tons (approximately 17 million kg) of the explosive TNT.

Within hours, the results of the test were relayed to President Harry S. Truman. At the time, Truman was in Potsdam, a city in Germany, which had surrendered to the Allies on May 2. Truman, who as vice president had assumed the presidency after Roosevelt's death on April 12, was attending a secret meeting with the British prime minister Winston Churchill and the Soviet premier Joseph Stalin. The president told Premier Stalin that the United States had a new weapon of devastating power, but he did not disclose the nature of the weapon. Stalin expressed his hope that the weapon would be used promptly and effectively against the Japanese. Churchill, of course, knew all about the bomb because British and American scientists had been working together on the project since 1942. In fact, Stalin knew much more about the bomb than he revealed. He and the military leaders of the Soviet Union had been receiving secret intelligence reports on the American and British efforts.

The Atomic Attack

United States officials alerted the Japanese government to the danger of the proposed atomic bombs. Their many warnings were ignored. On August 6, 1945, the Japanese city of Hiroshima was hit with the uranium bomb. The city was devastated. Killed and wounded numbered near 100,000.

Following the blast, the U.S. government issued many more warnings of possible future bombings and a request for peace negotiations, which included promises that the United States would maintain the position of the imperial Japanese family as rulers. The Japanese disregarded the

The uranium bomb was given "Little Boy" as a code name. (Courtesy of the U.S. National Archives and Records Administration)

warnings again. Three days after the uranium bomb exploded in Hiroshima, the plutonium bomb was dropped on Nagasaki. The Japanese surrendered five days later on August 14, 1945. A peace accord was signed aboard the battleship *Missouri* on September 2, 1945.

When Japan surrendered, the Japanese did not know that the United States had detonated the world's total stockpile of atomic weapons. Three bombs had been completed by August 1945. A plutonium bomb had been tested in July in New Mexico, and the others had been dropped on Japan in August. By September, none remained.

The difficult decision to employ nuclear weapons against Japan involved both military and political considerations. Military projections of Allied casualties during an invasion of the Japanese home islands were about 200,000 soldiers. One argument for using the atomic bomb, therefore, was that it would hopefully bring about immediate surrender and avoid such estimated bloodshed. The Allied commanders soon learned also that many young Japanese officers wanted to continue fighting even after the nuclear bombs had been dropped.

The political decision to bomb Japan also reflected a growing American distrust of Stalin and the government of the Soviet Union. President Truman's advisers persuaded him that a willingness to use nuclear weapons would give the United States a strong hand in the international settlements that followed the end of World War II.

The plutonium bomb detonates above the Japanese city, Nagasaki, in 1945. (Courtesy of the National Archives and Records Administration)

6

The Aftermath of Nuclear War

In the late 1930s before World War II, newspapers and magazines carried an occasional story about atomic science, and the public was vaguely aware of the mysterious properties of radium and actinium and other radioactive materials. News of the atom bomb and its power, however, came as a major surprise in 1945 because of the secrecy that had covered all the steps leading to the release of nuclear energy. When the news came out, it was evident to the public that scientists had played a major role in achieving a victorious outcome to the largest war ever fought. In addition to the bomb, major advances in electronics and computer science gave the public reason to be pleased with the role that scientists had played. Such public approval gave scientists more political influence than they had ever had before.

The level of information that should be provided to the public about the atomic bomb program was a matter of controversy. On one side were those who wished to keep secret as much information as possible about both the science and the technology of bomb-making. However, Lieutenant General Leslie Groves, among others, was convinced that future public policy should rest on some base of knowledge about how the bomb project had been carried out. In addition, he sought to give credit to those who had done the scientific work—and to take some credit himself for the successful management of such a large and complicated endeavor.

Groves had been preparing all along for the moment at which the story of the Manhattan Project could be told. Henry D. Smyth, one of the physicists on the Chicago team, had—since 1942—been designated by Groves as the official historian of the overall project. Smyth had maintained a running account of each step. Consequently, just seven days after the bomb was dropped on Hiroshima, a detailed report authored by Smyth was ready for distribution. The report contained information on the functions of uranium 235 and plutonium in the explosive fission reaction. There was even some discussion of the procedures used at Oak Ridge to separate the uranium 235 from the uranium 238. Many people saw this report as potentially very helpful to the scientists and technicians of other countries who might be trying to put together their own nuclear weapons.

Relations between the United States and the Soviet Union were not cordial even though they were allies against Germany during the war. After the war, the Soviet occupation of Poland and the Balkan countries and threats of a Soviet-backed revolution in Greece caused more tension. Nevertheless, a large number of the scientists and some political leaders saw the report as an opening for negotiation with the Soviet Union rather than confrontation. In any case, President Truman had different ideas. At a news briefing in October 1945, Truman revealed that the policy of the United States would be to withhold all further information about nuclear weapons—both from allies and potential opponents. Truman adopted the position that the United States should maintain a monopoly on such weapons for as long as possible.

In the meantime, Smyth's fame spread because of the importance of the report he had written. In time, he was appointed to prestigious positions in the U.S. government and to an ambassadorship to the atomic agency of the United Nations.

Policy Consequences

High officials of government including leaders of the armed forces recognized the key contributions of science and engineering to the war effort. Before the war, government engagement in science had been sparse. After the war, far broader and deeper engagements were contemplated. In the late 1940s, strong efforts were launched to find ways to retain the services of the scientists and technologists who were leaving government service to return to their prewar occupations. However, there were few established procedures within the federal government for hiring large numbers of scientists, and there were no organizations set up to manage scientific research programs.

The scientists' attitudes were also changing dramatically. Before World War II, most scientists were not enthusiastic about government involvement in research. Leaders in the various scientific fields were almost unanimous in their belief that government sponsorship of research meant bureaucratic interference. Postwar attitudes had softened after the vast majority of scientists had some actual experience with working for one or another government agency—including the armed forces. Many scientists came to believe that arrangements could be made with the government to financially support scientific research without damaging the independence of individual scientists and without bending the direction of the research effort.

ORGANIZATIONAL ARRANGEMENTS

Three major options were available to planners and officials within the government and the military services for retaining scientific expertise. These options all held promise of assuring continuing scientific progress related to public goals. One such option was the so-called think tank arrangement. Under this option, a new corporation was established in the same way that any new business is. However, the charter for these new

*Members of President Dwight D. Eisenhower's Science Advisory
Commission were photographed soon after Eisenhower's Atoms for Peace
speech at the United Nations. Nine of the 18 members were physicists.*
(Courtesy of the Lawrence Berkeley National Laboratory)

kinds of corporations specified that the company was not to be
operated to make a profit. Consequently, such companies were
called not-for-profit corporations. Among the first of such
organizations to be started was the RAND Corporation. The
founders included several universities, the Ford Foundation,
the Douglas Aircraft Company, and the U.S. Air Force. One of
the advantages for the RAND officials was that because it was
not a government agency it could recruit and hire scientists
without the restrictions of civil service regulations.

A second option was to create a unit of government that
could work effectively with existing civilian organizations that
employed large numbers of scientists. Mainly, such existing
civilian organizations were colleges and universities, but a
number of private firms were started after World War II with

the sole mission to provide scientific and technical services to government agencies under contractual agreements.

Government agencies had, of course, purchased goods and services from civilian organizations since the country was founded. However, there were specific problems involved in the purchase of scientific and engineering services. For example, there was no good way to measure the quality or the quantity of the services to be provided. Contractors could charge the government for the hours worked by various levels of employees, but there was no way of knowing how productive the workers were during those hours. If the nature of the work was "thinking scientific thoughts," what was the product? Consequently, new approaches were needed that rested on the good faith and goodwill of the people who entered into these contractual agreements.

Such an approach was taken in the creation of the Office of Naval Research (ONR) in 1946. The main idea was that ONR would provide a strong link between the technical segments of the navy and the scientists in colleges and universities across the country. The principal tool for accomplishing this objective was the grant-in-aid. This idea was borrowed from philanthropic organizations such as the Rockefeller Foundation. In effect, the grant money that passed from a government agency such as the ONR to a university was a gift with no strings attached. Such a gift might support a line of research at the university for several years. No one from the government came around to see whether the original goal set by the scientist's grant request was being achieved. In fact, many times research workers found that their initial ideas were not fruitful and greatly changed lines of research had to be laid out well after the grant had been awarded. There was no penalty for such changes. At the end of the grant period, however, an assessment was made by an assembly of other scientists regarding the quality of the effort. If it was judged deficient, no further support would be forthcoming.

Arrangements that copied those of the ONR were made by other units of government to provide broad support of science. One such organization was the National Science Foundation (NSF). When it was launched in 1950, several of the people who had helped manage ONR were brought into the new organization to make sure that proper procedures were followed and that the independence of the scientists who received grants would not be compromised. The ONR model was also followed to a large degree in the creation of the National Institutes of Health, which now provides grant support for research in the biomedical sciences.

Finally, the third option for building permanent connections between the government and scientists was the maintenance of national laboratories. The national laboratories are called GOCOs, which stands for government owned-contractor operated. The Manhattan Project first created the blueprint for such arrangements on a large scale. In the area of nuclear science, the GOCO, in the form of national laboratories, has been the main organizational arrangements over the post-World War II years.

From the Manhattan Project to the Atomic Energy Commission

General Groves's goal in the postwar period was to keep at least a semblance of the basic research and development capability intact. The practical objective was to create a modest stockpile of plutonium weapons to be used mainly as political assets in the postwar negotiations over control of the territories that had been occupied by Germany and Japan at the height of the war. General Groves and other high military commanders saw nuclear weapons as the tools that would forestall Soviet expansion, for example. However, few people realized the level of effort that would be required to assemble as many as five or six such weapons over the next 18 months.

Tensions between the United States and the Soviet Union continued to increase month by month. Each country tried to obstruct the international activities of the other. It was a form of war without the clash of armies. Consequently, the concept of a "cold war" between the United States and the Soviet Union was formulated. This idea provided a new incentive for weapon development. While the strategic military needs based on such a concept seemed clear, national policies regarding the use of atomic power were ill defined. History provided no precedents for the management of such awesome powers. In particular, a basic question was whether civilian or military authorities would have custody of the actual bombs. An even larger question was who would dominate the decisions about continuing development of nuclear weapons and the programs for the application of nuclear power.

In these matters, there was a partial answer in the traditions of governance in the United States. That tradition held that civilian authority was always to be paramount. This was the line taken by President Truman, who addressed the issue in January 1946—just five months after the Japanese surrender.

The questions were important enough to require special legislation at the national level, and Truman called for the elected representatives in Congress to act. At the time, a bill had been brought forward in the House of Representatives that would have established strict military control of weapons and their development—with harsh penalties for the disclosure of atomic secrets. Truman was not enthusiastic about this bill.

At the same time, a special panel was established in the Senate under a first-term senator, Brien McMahon of Connecticut. His counterpart in the House of Representatives was Congresswoman Helen Douglas of California. Together, they crafted a bill that gave responsibility for nuclear energy development to a five-member commission composed entirely of civilians. The atomic scientists strongly favored this bill. Their public backing of the McMahon bill and their protests against crippling amendments helped achieve passage of the bill into law as the Atomic Energy Act in August 1946. As a result, the Atomic Energy Commission (AEC) was established to replace the Manhattan Project.

In order to clarify the military's role, a second law, the National Security Act of 1947, was soon passed. This statute provided the means for a continuation of military influence on public policy and the operation of the various nuclear systems. One feature was the establishment of the Armed Forces Special Weapons Project. This new project allowed military leaders to influence the design of advanced weapons and supervise their transfer to operational military formations such as air force squadrons. It also assured the means to provide security clearances for workers and to enforce the secrecy rules.

Regarding the pursuit of basic nuclear science, the situation was confusing. On one side, there was no apparent need for additional basic research to foster weapon development. However, most political leaders were convinced of the value of basic nuclear research—indeed, of research in all aspects of the physical sciences. Likewise, such basic, theory-related research had wide support from the voters. Consequently, the idea of expanding the national laboratories where scientists could study all aspects of nuclear energy gained momentum. Facilities in California, Washington State, Utah, Nevada, New Mexico, Iowa, and Long Island, New York, were upgraded to the status of permanent, federally funded facilities. This expansion came with many twists and turns.

Los Alamos and Its Offspring

In the beginning, Los Alamos Laboratory was managed by the Army Corps of Engineers. Shortly after the laboratory's founding, however, its administration was transferred to the University of California. This arrangement helped disguise the nature of the research and development program there. It also made the job of recruiting top-level scientists easier. The university as an employer was more attractive to scientists than either the government, in general, or the military, in particular.

When the war ended, the scientists at Los Alamos were worried that their work could not be appreciated by the wider community because it was so secretive. These worries turned out to be groundless. With their jobs completed at Los Alamos, many of the scientists were offered excellent positions by academic institutions and industrial firms that recognized the quality of the research talents that had been gathered there. This situation caused problems for General Groves and others. While the need for pure science and some of the other functions at Los Alamos did decline for a short period, the related work of continuing bomb production soon became as urgent as it had been during the war.

The first three atom bombs had been literally handmade by the scientists and engineers at Los Alamos. Building a stockpile of such bombs, however, required a different approach. For example, some specific engineering effort was needed to reduce the excess weight of the bombs. Much more emphasis on standardization of parts was also needed so that assembly could be regularized.

The mesa at Los Alamos was surrounded by steep canyon walls and could not be expanded to accommodate a bomb factory. Moreover, the scientific staff was not sympathetic to mass-producing bombs. Most of the workers at Los Alamos were mainly interested in research and looked forward to careers in colleges or universities. Consequently, in the interests of efficiency and morale, advanced design and production was moved to a better location.

The single unit that had been Los Alamos divided. A daughter unit, called the Sandia National Laboratories, formed in

1945. It was located on the outskirts of Albuquerque, New Mexico, about 100 miles (160 km) from Los Alamos.

The regents of the University of California were reluctant to expand their area of responsibility to encompass what was to be a weapons design and production factory because such work was not suited to academic administrators. After an intense study, the administrative and managerial functions for the Sandia National Laboratories were turned over to Bell Laboratories, Inc., a subsidiary of American Telephone and Telegraph Company (AT&T) in late 1949. In a legal sense, AT&T acted as a trustee for the Atomic Energy Commission. The contract with the U.S. government called for Bell Laboratories to provide administrative services and management guidance with no profit and no fee. However, the executives at Bell Laboratories believed that the Bell organization would benefit by working on the most advanced electronic systems that would be used in the fabrication of atomic bombs. This arrangement later provided a precedent for other government actions that brought the capabilities of large organizations into activities that generated no profits. Not-for-profit arrangements became a common means for the government to acquire scientific and technical talent without expanding the federal bureaucracy.

SYSTEMS ENGINEERING

An important by-product of the arrangements with Bell Laboratories was the introduction of a well-structured philosophy of systems design and development. This new approach established what were called "functional requirements" as design and development goals. In other words, systems were expected to meet the needs and expectations of the users of such systems—rather than the needs and expectations of the design engineers. In addition, the results of field testing and user evaluation were fed back into the design process as specific corrective instructions. For example, if the design of the external casing for an atom bomb did not match the equipment used to lift the bomb into the body of the aircraft for delivery to a target, the precise deficiency would be documented and communicated back to the design engineers so that the deficiency would be corrected. As time went on, this philosophy spread widely throughout the community of design engineers in all areas, including aircraft and computer design. Elements of this system are now incorporated in the development of civilian products such as automobiles and kitchen appliances under the term *user-friendly* design.

Argonne National Laboratory

Even before the end of of the war, there were crowding problems at the Metallurgical Laboratory that was part of the University of Chicago. When Fermi and his colleagues achieved the first sustained and controlled chain reaction in an unused squash court behind and beneath the grandstand at the University of Chicago football stadium, some of the workers raised questions of safety for themselves and the unwitting people who lived nearby.

Various sites around the southern rim of the city of Chicago were surveyed. Arthur Holly Compton, a physicist and the director of the Metallurgical Laboratory, discovered an attractive site a few miles southwest of the Chicago city limits. The space included areas set aside for camping and outdoor recreation and a forest preserve. The preserve was owned by the county government and was called Argonne Forest.

Army officials arranged for the county to lease the ground to the University of Chicago, and some of the reactor materials were transferred to the new location. A new reactor was built on the site using heavy water rather than graphite as the moderator in order to compare the rate of neutron generation.

However, as the war began to wind down, the site—then known as the Argonne Laboratory—had to be abandoned. Long-term lease arrangements were rejected by the county government.

University officials found an alternative site in an adjacent county and purchased property south of the town of Downers Grove. Oddly, in spite of the forced change in location, the facility retained the old name of Argonne National Laboratory.

The long-term mission of the Argonne Laboratory was determined by the pioneering work on reactor research there. In a sense, all atomic power plants are reactors, descendants of the machine first built on the University of Chicago campus. At the Argonne site during the early postwar years, scientists tested dozens of variants in fuel composition, cooling techniques, shielding materials, and safety devices for atomic reactors.

Atomic energy seemed to promise pollution-free electricity generation at this time, and much practical research was needed to support decisions about atomic power-plant development. However, by the early 1950s, the scientists at Argonne were not satisfied with conducting entirely practical research. Consequently, they initiated more theory-based research into the fundamental properties of atomic nuclei. As time passed, the scientists expanded into many other areas of study as well. For example, Argonne National Laboratory also became a center for research on the properties of materials at extremely low temperatures.

From the Radiation Laboratory to the Lawrence Berkeley Laboratory

In California, similar developments were under way. The technique developed by Ernest Lawrence and his colleagues to separate uranium isotopes used Lawrence's machine, the cyclotron. Uranium atoms, in the form of a gas made of uranium and fluorine, were accelerated in special cyclotrons called calutrons. The gaseous molecules were propelled to high speed, and the lighter uranium 235 was pushed onto a higher path than the heavier uranium 238. This method for sorting the uranium isotopes turned out to be very wasteful but was successful in producing useful quantities of uranium 235. Large versions of the calutron accelerators were installed at Oak Ridge in Tennessee in 1943.

Meanwhile, the cyclotrons at the Radiation Laboratory on the campus of the University of California at Berkeley continued to be used to produce radioactive isotopes of chemicals that were important in biological processes. For example, one product was radioactive iodine, which is taken up by the thyroid gland, in the throat. The thyroid gland regulates growth, and its malfunction can lead to a condition known as goiter, in which the gland becomes greatly swollen. A Geiger counter will reveal the presence of radioactive iodine in the thyroid gland. Doctors can then analyze the rate that the thyroid absorbs the iodine and make specific diagnoses. Moreover, the radioactive iodine can be used to irradiate and destroy cancer of the thyroid because it is drawn to that organ.

Scientists also use cyclotron accelerators to study the internal structure of atoms and subatomic particles. During the war, this area of research was put aside so that skilled personnel could focus on war-related work. However, after the war, basic research functions were reinstated and the laboratory was renamed the Lawrence Berkeley National Laboratory.

General Expansion

Los Alamos gave birth to Sandia National Laboratories but continued to exist in its own right and eventually expanded until there were more than 7,000 workers there. Sandia, in turn, gave birth to Livermore National Laboratory, which began as a site for research on explosives and combustion chemistry and ended up as a lead research facility in the study of human biology. At its foundation, it was managed by the General Research Corporation, a holding company for patents that were assigned to faculty members for their research there. In 1950, the new facility was renamed the Lawrence Livermore National Laboratory and management was transferred to the University of California.

Early in the postwar period, the scientists who worked in colleges and universities in the eastern United States were disappointed at the lack of a large atomic research facility in their region. They persuaded academic officials to band together and offer the Atomic Energy Commission the opportunity to encourage nuclear research in the neighborhood of some of the most highly regarded institutions in the country, such as Harvard, Yale, the Massachusetts Institute of Technology (MIT), and Johns Hopkins, to name but a few. The upshot was the 1947 creation of the Brookhaven National Laboratory on Long Island, about 60 miles (about 100 km) east of New York City.

The two large production sites, Oak Ridge and the large facility near Hanford, in Washington State, also evolved their own basic research arms. A small research unit called the Clinton Laboratory had been located near the production units at Oak Ridge since 1943. This unit merged with the main facility in 1946 so that the name Oak Ridge National Laboratory became accurate. In addition, the directors of the installation encouraged regional institutions of higher education to band together. These institutions formed a group known as the Oak Ridge Associated Universities. This arrangement permitted exchanges of resources including, for example, work-study opportunities for students from low-income families.

The Hanford facility in Washington was in many ways the most industrial of all the atomic development centers. Its highly focused function was the production of plutonium by the irradiation of uranium in large reactors. However, the senior people responsible for operating the facility believed that they deserved to participate in a wider range of activities, including both basic and applied research. Their wishes were realized with the founding of a new unit nearby called the Pacific Northwest Laboratory. This facility was managed by Battelle Memorial Institute, a not-for-profit scientific and technical organization with headquarters in Columbus, Ohio.

Overall Trends

The organizations put together hurriedly under the pressures of the wartime emergency might well have been dismembered when the war was over. However, the growing rivalry with the Soviet Union, the onset of further national emergencies such as the Korean War and the war in Vietnam, and the government's general reluctance to terminate successful enterprises all led to the continuation of these organizations. In fact, more organizations do nuclear research under government sponsorship now than in 1945.

According to a review compiled by the U.S. Department of Energy—which now funds all the national laboratories as well as other research enterprises—there are in the United States nine multiprogram laboratories (such as Los Alamos), 10 single-purpose laboratories (such as the Fermi National Accelerator Laboratory [Fermilab] near Chicago), and six specific mission laboratories (such as the Stanford Synchrotron Radiation Laboratory run by Stanford University in Palo Alto, California). The total staff size for all these facilities is around 70,000 people, none of whom are directly employed by the government as civil servants. All these staff members work for contractors such as the University of California or the Battelle Memorial Institute.

In addition to sheer growth in size, the national laboratory system has tended to grow in scope as well. The subject matter of the research being done has diversified greatly. For example an initial concern with the safety of workers exposed to radiation led to a strong interest in the medical conditions of people exposed to radiation. Some scientists expected large number of mutations to appear in the children of Hiroshima and Nagasaki survivors. Field research revealed fewer mutation than predicted in such children. However, scientists lacked the ability to scan genes at the molecular level. Their uncertainty about what radiation did to genetic material led the nuclear researchers to spread their interests to include studies of the detailed composition of genes.

Atomic physics opened many other lines of research. For example, nuclear tests generated thousands of numerical measurements. Making sense of these numbers required the use of elaborate mathematics. The calculations needed to solve the equations were very laborious and time-consuming. Consequently, it made sense for the leaders at the Atomic Energy Commission to support mathematical research and the development of high-speed electronic computers.

In sum, after World War II a very elaborate network of scientific research and engineering facilities arose around the initial centers at Los Alamos, Oak Ridge, Hanford, and Argonne. Each of these facilities took on new life, new personnel, new equipment, and new scientific directions as the postwar era unfolded. Although all the centers receive their support from single agency of the federal government, the actual management of the research programs and projects is highly decentralized. Each national laboratory director has much independence with only general guidance from the federal government.

European Counterparts

While World War II was still under way, the Soviet Union did not have the resources to achieve the high level of nuclear research or weapons development created in the United States. However, soon after the war was over, Soviet leaders commanded the construction of a string of research and production facilities in the far reaches of Siberia. These sites were even more shut off from the rest of the society than were Oak Ridge or Hanford in the United States.

In England, the Cavendish Laboratory never ceased to conduct fundamental, theoretically oriented research. Applied research on systems other than weapons—mainly atomic energy–fueled power plants—was started in the early 1950s at the Atomic Energy Research Establishment at Harwell in the region near Oxford. During the war when the focus was on weapons development, the site was occupied by military personnel—specifically members of the Royal Air Force. After the war, the facility was enlarged and staffed by civilians.

The Harwell facility is roughly comparable to the Argonne National Laboratory in the United States. Postwar, the focus was on power-plant development, and the main tool was a uranium-fueled reactor using heavy water as a moderator rather than graphite.

A typical problem in the early stages of power-plant development involved the design of the metal tubes containing the nuclear fuel. Specifically, the engineers at Harwell developed methods for the identification of fractures or flaws in long sections of pipe. A radiant energy source is sent along the inside of the pipe, while a radiation detector keeps pace along the outside. Variations in the volume of radiation coming through the walls of the pipe reveal flaws in the pipe walls.

Most of the production and distribution of the various radioactive isotopes used in Great Britain for medical and industrial purposes comes from Harwell. Meanwhile, the role of the Harwell scientists in the independent development of nuclear weapons is still shrouded in secrecy.

The Council of Ministers in London has the official authority for administering the full array of atomic facilities including reactors and electric power plants in Great Britain. This body carries out the functions that were assigned to the Atomic Energy Commission and that are now handled by the Department of Energy in the United States.

In France, Frédéric Joliot-Curie's research collaboration with his wife, Irène, was revitalized after the war. The liberation government of France under Charles de Gaulle supported their research; however, resources were scarce and progress was sporadic. The pair had to build a new laboratory from the ground up in an abandoned military installation called Fort de Châtillon on the outskirts of Paris.

The French research goal was similar to that of the British to develop reactors to produce electricity on a large scale. The Joliot-Curies and their crew constructed several reactors similar to those built at the Hanford site in the United States. Such reactors produce weapons-grade plutonium, a fact noted by French government officials who hoped to produce atomic bombs, increasing France's power on the world stage.

Irène and Frédéric Joliot-Curie were both communists. The position of the Communist Party in France and elsewhere was determined by officials of the Soviet government in Moscow. The party position at that time was opposed to the construction of atom bombs under any circumstances. Consequently, the Joliot-Curies strongly disagreed with high government officials who wanted to build a bomb. In 1950, the French prime minister Georges Bidault dismissed Frédéric from government employ. His laboratory was taken over by scientists and engineers from the Corps des Mines—a very powerful French government agency. An engineer named Pierre Guilaumant was named director of the laboratory, and Francis Henri Perrin, the son of French Nobel Prize winner Jean-Baptiste Perrin, was named chief scientist. The first French atomic bomb was detonated in a test firing in the Sahara Desert in February 1960. The French continue to develop and install nuclear power plants for electricity production, making France one of the world leaders in the use of atomic energy.

CERN

All western European countries were short of financial resources for some years after World War II. Consequently, as individual nations they could not hope to support the level of basic research in nuclear science that was proceeding in the United States. The alternative was some form of collective enterprise. Serious discussions about a joint effort to build a nuclear research laboratory began in the late 1940s. By the early 1950s, a site was identified on the border between France and Switzerland near the Swiss city of Geneva. By the mid-1950s, construction was under way on a very large, advanced cyclotron called a proton synchrotron. Built in an underground tunnel, it is a little more than one-third of a mile (about 700 m) in circumference.

The facility is called CERN, which is the abbreviation in French for the European Organization for Nuclear Research. Twelve European countries sponsored the construction and support the research efforts there. Scientists from these 12 and other countries are permitted to use the synchrotron to do their research. Guest scientists come from Japan, Russia, Turkey, and China. U.S. scientists have also asked and been given permission to use the machine because no exact duplicate of the CERN synchrotron exists in the United States.

The facility is dedicated entirely to basic research on the atomic nucleus. In this regard, the facility is most comparable to the installations at the Lawrence Berkeley National Laboratory, Brookhaven National Laboratory, and Fermilab in the United States.

7

The Hydrogen Bomb
or Atoms for Peace —
or Both

When World War II ended, it was evident that the relationship between the United States and Great Britain on one side and the Soviet Union on the other was changing; already there had been a number of disputes among the Allies. Instead of the limited partnership that was arranged during World War II, the cold war arose. New military alliances such as the North Atlantic Treaty Organization (NATO) formed to oppose the Soviet Union and other countries in eastern Europe under Soviet domination.

These political antagonisms meant that secrecy about atomic technology needed to continue; however, high U.S. government officials were strongly motivated to make it appear that the United States was not dedicated to using weapons of mass destruction. In short, U.S. leaders wanted to keep a monopoly on atomic weapons but reassure the world that the United States would never use such weapons.

International Control Fails and Anxiety Increases

From the moment that the first nuclear weapon was successfully tested, there were individuals who called for international agreements to eliminate or at least limit atomic bombs and other nuclear weapons. The group included some of the very scientists who had helped develop the weapons. Finding ways to reduce the threat was also an immediate topic for the General Assembly of the United Nations (U.N.), which had been chartered before the war ended. In January 1946, the first resolution passed by the assembly created the International Atomic Energy Commission (IAEC). Its job was to seek international agreements to restrict the development and spread of nuclear weapons. The commission was set up under the direction of the Security Council, the executive arm of the United Nations.

The discharge of the Soviet Union's first atomic bomb in September 1949 and a similar test by the British in October 1952 made obvious the IAEC's lack of success. By that time, the IAEC had already been disbanded. It was clear to the world's diplomats that some other approach was needed.

On a more mundane level, when the scientists and military leaders of the Soviet Union ignited their first nuclear device in 1949, many people in the United States became acutely fearful that a nuclear war would breakout between the United States and the Soviet Union. Schoolchildren practiced bomb drills in which they were taught to hide under their desks. Prosperous families built bomb shelters stocked with food and medical supplies in their basements and backyards.

The political climate became more and more confusing. Many scientists and popular leaders advocated direct negotiations with the Soviet Union that might lead to an agreement to prohibit nuclear weapons altogether. Others advocated more intense efforts in the United States to stay ahead of the Soviets in nuclear science and the development of atomic weapons.

The Super Bomb

The idea that a bomb could be made that would release the energies of atomic fusion rather than the energies of fission had been circulating in scientific circles for some years prior to World War II. During the war, as early as 1943, Los Alamos scientists gave serious attention to the prospect of a so-called super bomb, based on nuclear fusion. The concept behind such a bomb was even simpler and more widely understood than that of the atom, or fission, bomb. Fusion occurs when two relatively light atoms—hydrogen, deuterium, or lithium—merge to form helium. The amount of energy given off by this reaction exceeds the energy of fission by hundreds of times. The problem is that an enormous input of energy is needed to force the nuclei of atoms to merge, so the key was to use an atomic bomb to set off a hydrogen bomb. There are three stages in the detonation of the super bomb, first, conventional explosives drive sections of metallic plutonium together to reach a critical mass; second, the plutonium ignites in a sphere around a core of concentrated hydrogen/lithium or related material; third, the hydrogen and lithium atoms merge. For a few very small fractions of a second, the heat generated by the third ignition exceeds the temperature of the Sun.

Edward Teller was the forceful advocate for the development of the hydrogen bomb. (Courtesy of the Lawrence Berkeley National Laboratory)

Edward Teller is generally credited with pushing the hydrogen bomb project to a successful conclusion. He was also instrumental in solving some of the major technical problems in the design of the bomb. The detailed work was carried out by the staff at Los Alamos, Sandia National Laboratories, and Lawrence Livermore National Laboratory.

It was not possible to test the super bomb within the confines of the continental United States because of the size of the explosion. Coral atolls in the Pacific Ocean were used for such tests. After a hydrogen bomb was successfully detonated on an islet in the Eniwetok circle, the director of the Atomic Energy Commission sent a key message to President Dwight D. Eisenhower on October 31, 1952. It read, "The Island of Elugelal is missing."

For a brief period, American politicians and national security experts believed that the United States had regained superiority over the Soviets in weapon power and that the gap could not be closed. However, the Soviets not only closed the gap in weapon power but moved ahead in delivery capabilities. This fact was dramatically demonstrated in 1957 when the Soviets were able to put a satellite called Sputnik into orbit. Again, the futility of trying to enclose science and technology in a shroud of secrecy was revealed.

The Demise of J. Robert Oppenheimer

High in the ranks of government, in the federal legislature, in organizations such as the U.S. Atomic Energy Commission, and in military and secret intelligence organizations, there was a sense of defeat when it was learned that the Soviet Union already possessed nuclear weapons in 1949. Experts felt guilty for predicting that such a situation would never happen or that it would require much more time than it did. Some of the blame could be directed toward actual spies such as Klaus

Fuchs, who had been a member of the Los Alamos team but was exposed by British intelligence, tried in their courts, convicted, and jailed for espionage in 1950.

The main problem was that most of the high officials did not realize that science cannot be made secret for any significant length of time. All the scientific knowledge needed to build an atomic bomb was widely published in the 1930s. Some of this knowledge required verification—as was done by Enrico Fermi at the University of Chicago; however, the construction of an atom bomb did not require much more science than was already available. So rather than more science, the missing elements were really only the investment of vast public resources to produce pure uranium 235 and pure plutonium and the engineering effort to translate the scientific concepts into practical working models. Consequently, most historians now believe that the role of Soviet espionage was relatively minor in the success of the Soviet bomb program. At that moment, nevertheless, highly placed people in the United States sought to shift the blame for their mistaken assumptions onto others.

The most prominent person to be made such a scapegoat was Robert Oppenheimer. The particular action that aroused hostility was Oppenheimer's reluctance to push for the super bomb. Oppenheimer's reluctance came about after the decision to go ahead with the development of the hydrogen bomb had already been made, so his opposition was more symbolic than effective. His position, however, provided an excuse for those who resented him or were disturbed by his historical sympathies with communist causes.

He was called before a congressional committee and cross-examined about his relationships with some friends and relatives who were members or who had been members of the Communist Party. Since he had committed no legal offense—and, in fact, was still regarded as a hero by most people who were aware of his work—the penalty imposed was the removal of his security clearances. Afterward, he could no longer serve as a participant or adviser on the decision-making bodies that were responsible for nuclear policy in the United States. He could not even read some of his own reports because they were classified as secret. Altogether, Oppenheimer's persecution was an unfortunate episode in the workings of the U.S. government.

While officially disgraced, Oppenheimer was still respected by the majority of his peers. He joined the staff of the Center for Advanced Studies (CAS) at Princeton University in 1953. His status as a national figure was partly restored in 1963 when President Lyndon B. Johnson awarded Oppenheimer the Fermi medal for scientific distinction. Oppenheimer died while still associated with the CAS in 1966.

Additional Uses for Nuclear Energy

Some people who were distressed and depressed by the application of atomic science to weapons development sought to balance that negative with some positive alternatives. Some who were optimists saw nuclear energy as the means of achieving a condition approaching utopia on Earth. As a counterweight to concerns about the spread of atomic weapons, in the 1950s leading scientists such as Glenn Seaborg presented the citizenry of the United States with a glowing view of future marvels that would come from atomic energy. At the top of the list of alternative uses for nuclear energy were electric power plants. Next were engines for submarines and other naval vessels. Both these ideas materialized as working technologies, but there were some far more fantastic ideas that were seriously considered by experts as well as promoters and politicians.

One of the most intriguing of these ideas was the proposal for a nuclear propulsion system for either large aircraft or spacecraft or both. The need for heavy shielding between the reactor and the crew killed this concept: The weight of such shielding and the need to maintain some distance between the reactor and the human crew meant that such a craft could never carry passengers. The advantage to such an idea was the possibility that it could stay airborne for long periods of time, but the technique of midair refueling perfected in 1957 made this advantage irrelevant. It was also obvious that military mission requirements could be fulfilled much more easily by multi-engine jet aircraft and intercontinental ballistic missiles.

Other prospective uses of nuclear power included mining, the construction of canals, the creation of underground storage caverns for holding petroleum or natural gas supplies, spaceship propulsion, and the desalination of water. All these projects had some merit but foundered on economic factors and the threat of radioactive contamination.

SUBMARINE PROPULSION

Of the two practical applications of nuclear energy that were relatively successful, the submarine propulsion system was the first to be brought to fruition. The key figure in the rapid development of this idea was a senior naval officer, Hyman Rickover.

During World War II, Rickover served as the administrative head of all the electronics development efforts in the navy. With this background, it was not surprising that he was among a select few chosen to attend the first formal training school for nuclear applications studies at the Oak Ridge nuclear facility. The school opened in August 1946, just a year after the war ended. The first course was attended by more than 50 students from varied backgrounds. There were four other naval officers in attendance in addition to Rickover. He was the senior officer in the group and was able to bond the others into a team that would hold together for many years. This team, with Rickover in the lead, would go on to direct the development of the nuclear navy.

Rickover persuaded the top leaders of the navy—and important civilians in government including members of Congress—that a special unit of the navy's Bureau of Ships should be created to exploit nuclear propulsion systems. He was put in charge of this unit and promoted to admiral in 1948. At the same time, he persuaded the directors of the AEC to establish a unit that would coordinate reactor development for ship propulsion. He was named to head this unit also. Consequently, in 1948, Rickover occupied two crucial positions: director of the navy's nuclear power branch and director of the AEC's naval reactors branch. From these positions he was able to direct a flow of funds into projects such as the design of a compact, well-shielded power plant. He chose the engineers at the Westinghouse company in Pittsburgh, Pennsylvania, to do this work.

The specific design included a nuclear reactor that generated steam to drive a turbine that was connected by a set of gears

Pressurized-Water Nuclear Propulsion System Layout

The nuclear power plant for a submarine uses the same flow of steam to spin two turbines: one to drive the propeller and one to drive an electric generator.

to the propeller shaft. The steam that drove the first turbine was then diverted to a second turbine connected to an electrical generator. This generator supplied electrical power for all the ship's functions and was also used to charge a bank of batteries that provided a reserve source of electricity in case of emergencies.

The design of this specialized power plant was initiated in 1950. The first atomic-powered submarine, the USS *Nautilus,* was launched in January 1954 at the completion of an amazingly short development period. In 1958, the *Nautilus* became the first submarine to travel underwater from one side of the polar ice cap to the other without surfacing.

Rickover was particularly sensitive to the safety problem. He realized that if there were a major malfunction aboard the submarine while it was cruising underwater, the submarine might disappear without a trace—taking a crew of more than 60 naval personnel to their death. In the political setting of the time, such an event might have led to a complete halt to the nuclear submarine program. Consequently, Rickover was extremely careful to make sure that the design of the total system was foolproof, that each mechanical part was of the highest quality, and that the crew members were trained to their utmost capabilities. He would not permit any participant in the program to cut corners. His rigidity in such matters angered some people, but in contrast to the experiences of other countries with nuclear submarine fleets, the U.S. Navy has had no serious reactor malfunctions aboard ship. There were some minor accidents aboard nuclear ships but none that was caused by a nuclear system itself.

During and after Rickover's tenure, the U.S. Navy acquired well over 70 nuclear submarines. During the height of the cold war, the U.S. fleet included 95 such submarines; however, because of the end of the cold war, cost cutting, and international disarmament agreements, this submarine armada is to be reduced to 50 vessels.

In addition, the U.S. Navy has also commissioned eight nuclear aircraft carriers and four nuclear missile cruisers. One nuclear cargo/supply ship was built for a civilian project with the help of a government subsidy. It was operated by a private company but was retired early, because it could not compete economically with ships of the same size that used oil for fuel.

ELECTRICAL POWER PLANTS

Immediately following World War II, the sole purpose for constructing nuclear reactors was to produce plutonium for use in weapons. Gradually, however, the idea that reactors could be designed to produce electric power began to take hold. By the early 1950s, several of the research and development centers within the Atomic Energy Commission built small reactors that could produce steam, which in turn could drive turbines attached to electric generators. Among the first was one, at the Oak Ridge National Laboratory, that produced enough electricity to activate four lightbulbs. A large increase in size was needed if such systems were to be adopted by the major public power companies.

Scaling up was done cautiously. Prototype reactors of gradually increasing size were constructed at the Argonne National Laboratory and at the Hanford site, among others. The design concept was not particularly complicated. Radioactivity generates heat. The heat can be used to make steam, and the steam can drive a turbine attached to an electric generator. It is necessary to enclose the nuclear core and the primary heat transfer pipes in a thick-walled building so that no radioactive contamination can reach the environment. Such buildings are designed to contain a severe chemical explosion if any such incident should occur.

At first blush, the prospect of electric power from the use of radioactive materials such as fuels was seen as a major boon to humanity. At the instigation of President Eisenhower in

1953, the idea blossomed. Many people believed that such a source of electricity might bring economic advances around the globe. Commercial organizations in the United States saw domestic markets opening, as well as markets for the sale and delivery of complete power plants to the less-developed countries of the world. Profits from the sale of such facilities in the United States appeared to be possible, and the prospect of international sales made the idea even more appealing. Several large companies in the United States were capable of building and selling complete nuclear reactors. Organizations in England, France, and the Soviet Union also had such capabilities. Consequently, the competition between prospective vendors of nuclear power plants became intense.

The early competition centered on some of the basic features of reactor design, particularly the methods used to control or moderate the pace of the nuclear reaction and the means used to cool the reactor core. One of the most popular types is a pressurized-water reactor, a scaled-up version of the power plant used in naval vessels, without the propulsion link. A major advantage of the pressurized-water reactor is that the water heated in the core by the nuclear reaction also serves as the core coolant and is totally recirculated so that it never leaves the main containment structure.

Other alternative arrangements include boiling-water reactors, liquid metal reactors, and reactors using graphite to control the rate of nuclear radiation. One type of liquid metal reactor uses a nonnuclear metal to convey heat from the core to a steam boiler. These reactors are very efficient because they operate at a very high temperature.

After the assembly of several experimental reactors in order to test design options, the first commercial reactor was installed at Shippingport, Pennsylvania, by the Duquesne Light Company in 1957. It was a relatively small plant rated at 60 million watts.

This control room is typical of a modern nuclear power plant. (Courtesy of the U.S. Department of Energy)

The first few privately owned reactors were subsidized by the U.S. government. For safety reasons, those built during the late 1950s through to the late 1960s were designed to produce less than 400 million watts. Such a modest power output was calculated to be well below the upper limit for the containment of any meltdown of the core. In other words, while accidents were possible, no breaks in containment were likely to happen with these early designs.

Ten additional commercial plants were put into operation over the following 10 years. Five were boiling-water reactors, two were pressurized-water reactors, two were liquid metal, and one was graphite controlled. The largest of these commercial reactors was a pressurized-water reactor built for the Consolidated Edison Company in Buchanan, New York, in 1963. It was rated at 250 million watts.

Political Adjustments

All these developments took place with the support of the Atomic Energy Commission. However, the commission was subject to criticism because it promoted the advance of nuclear power development at the same time that it was responsible for the approval of plant safety plans and provisions. Some politicians saw this situation as a source of internal conflict within the AEC and so proposed that the government role in nuclear power be reorganized. With congressional support in 1975, President Gerald Ford split the AEC into two new bodies by presidential directive. One was the Energy Research and Development Administration (ERDA), which would be responsible for promoting the advance of nuclear power production. The second was the Nuclear Regulatory Commission,

The Diablo Canyon site for a nuclear power plant is controversial because of the possibility of an earthquake. (Courtesy of JLM Visuals, Grafton, Wis.)

which, as its name proclaims, would be responsible for regulating the industry and enforcing safety standards.

A few months later, after the election to the presidency of Jimmy Carter in 1976, a large-scale governmental reorganization replaced ERDA with the Department of Energy (DOE). This department now has responsibility for the development of all forms of energy production including renewable energy sources such as solar power.

During the 1960s and 1970s, this succession of government agencies encouraged the construction of nuclear power plants. By 1979, there were 107 nuclear power plants in operation in the United States. Some of these plants are rated at more than 1 billion watts.

By the late 1970s, there were six plants on which construction was incomplete and a few that had been taken out of service. Some of these plants were retired because they were partially worn out and were inefficient. Another retiree, however, was plant No. 2 at Three Mile Island in Pennsylvania. It was taken out of service because of a loss-of-coolant accident on March 28, 1979, and subsequent breakup of the nuclear core. The accident had several causes. The main cause was a failure on the part of the operators to recognize the loss of coolant water and to restore coolant flow from an alternative source. When the plant managers informed local, state, and federal officials of the accident, the reactions of these officials were not well organized.

Nuclear Accidents

There had been some worries about reactor safety before the events at Three Mile Island. These worries were partly based on at least two accidents in nuclear power plants that released radioactivity into the atmosphere before the Three Mile Island accident. The first of these occurred at the Windscale plant

The Three Mile Island power plant is near Harrisburg, Pennsylvania. The loss-of-coolant accident in the No. 2 unit brought about a halt in the development of new nuclear power facilities in the United States. (Courtesy of JLM Visuals, Grafton, Wis.)

near Sellafield, England. This plant was constructed in the mid-1940s on the northwest coast of England to produce plutonium for the British nuclear weapons program. Electricity production was a by-product.

The reactor was modeled after the first nuclear pile that Fermi had built in Chicago; that is, it was powered by uranium 238, used graphite as a control material, and was cooled by air. In October 1957, some of the graphite blocks caught fire. Before the fire could be contained, some of the metal boxes holding uranium powder were ruptured, and the nuclear material was distributed by the plumes of smoke from the fire.

Fear of contamination led the authorities to halt the consumption of milk from cows within a 100-mile (160-km) radius of the plant for a year after the accident. Millions of gallons of contaminated milk were dumped into the North Sea. People as far away as Lithuania on the Baltic Sea complained of exposure to increased levels of radiation.

In May 1958, there probably was a partial core meltdown at the Chalk River reactor in Canada. This incident has not been fully publicized because of military security restrictions. The reactor was part of a joint British and Canadian weapons program.

Also over the years prior to the Three Mile Island incident, many minor accidents were recorded at various sites in the United States and in western Europe. For example, in 1967 a fire broke out in the containment structure of a small reactor near Annan, Scotland. The result was a partial meltdown of the core. No one was killed, but some radioactive gases escaped into the outside atmosphere.

The scientists and technicians who monitor radiation levels in the atmosphere generally concur that the worst nuclear release situations have occurred in the former Soviet Union. The evidence is almost totally circumstantial, but it is believed, for example, that dozens of partially exhausted nuclear fuel rods and large pieces of the cores of nuclear reactors have been dumped by the Russians into the Barents Sea above the Arctic Circle.

The Future of Nuclear Power Plants in the United States

After the 1979 accident at Three Mile Island, there were more opponents to the expansion of nuclear power generation than there were advocates. Public opinion has played an important role in checking the growth of power plant production for safety reasons. Also, today the very public utility companies that own the generators and sell electricity to consumers are no longer enthusiastic about building additional plants. In part, the damper stems from restrictions imposed by the Nuclear Regulatory Commission after the accident. Also, the federal laws protecting such companies from lawsuits arising from property loss, injury, or death from a nuclear accident are not as strong as the power companies would like. The executives of electric power companies are aware that as many as 2,000 claimants were allowed to pursue damage suits against the Three Mile Island power company by a verdict of the U.S. Supreme Court in 1996.

In the aftermath of the Three Mile Island accident, the cleanup of the plant at reactor site No. 2 took more than 10 years and cost more than $1 billion. Debris and intensely radioactive liquid waste had to be transported in three stages from the plant site to a waste repository in southeast Utah. The liquid metal used for heat transference during normal plant operations was the most dangerous waste in the containment building, because it can burst into flame if exposed to water. This material was transported by truck in special shielded containers from the plant site to a treatment facility 20 miles (32 km) distant. At the treatment facility, chemical procedures made the liquid metal inactive. It was then diluted until it could be classified as low-level waste. This material and the other solids and liquids from the accident site, some of which was still highly radioactive, were loaded onto special trains, carried 2,500 miles (4,000 km) by rail, reloaded onto trucks in Utah, and carried to the final resting place.

The accident at Chernobyl in the Soviet Union in April 1986 was much more destructive than that at Three Mile Island. The Ukrainian reactor was destroyed by a steam explosion that lifted the roof off the container building and by a subsequent fire. The cause of the accident was a series of operator errors, equipment failures, and faulty communications among members of the technical staff and even among those assigned to fight the fire and rescue the workers. The immediate result was 31 worker fatalities. The long-range consequences included the complete evacuation of the surrounding area and the high occurrence of radiation diseases such as leukemia and other forms of cancer in the people living in the area at the time of the accident.

There are many forms of disease and injury engendered by contact with radioactive materials. For example, uranium decay produces radon, a radioactive gas. Exposure to this gas can result in lung cancer and other lung diseases. Plutonium is produced in small quantities by power plant reactors. Plutonium is very long lasting and can enter the body as a contaminant of food or drink or as dust in the air. Plutonium can cause cancer and might be a cause of birth defects.

Although many fear the consequences of such accidents, some continue to advocate the expansion of nuclear power facilities. These advocates point out that a well-run nuclear power plant does not pollute the atmosphere with materials that cause acid rain or global warming. They believe that designers and operators of these facilities have now learned to avoid malfunctions.

In fact, nuclear reactors can now be made almost foolproof. As soon as the temperature in the core nears as unsafe level, a special radioactive alloy that makes up the fuel rods begins to expand. This expansion allows the atoms in the radioactive fuel to move apart, slows the nuclear fission, and halts the danger of the disastrous, uncontrolled chain reaction. Although this safeguard has been developed, only one prototype reactor has been constructed. Contracts for the research and development of this reactor have been canceled because government officials fear adverse public opinion.

The possibility of using controlled nuclear fusion as a power source is an attractive alternative to the employment of nuclear fission. The process of fission requires the use of radioactive elements such as uranium. Fusion, on the other hand, employs nonradioactive hydrogen as a fuel and produces no nuclear waste. However, the process that gives the hydrogen bomb its great explosive power is very difficult to control. No one has been able to design a piece of equipment that can successfully contain a fusion reaction for more than an instant. In addition, the energy required to achieve the reaction is greater than the energy produced. Someday, however, the promise of nuclear fusion may be realized.

8

Nuclear Medicine

Nuclear medicine began with Röntgen's discovery of X-rays in 1895. This breakthrough greatly improved a physician's ability to diagnosis bone diseases. However, the technology was often adopted by amateurs and was easily misused. Technical progress was not very rapid, partly because the orientation of most doctors was toward organic rather than mechanical knowledge.

An alternative to X-rays became available in 1896 when Antoine-Henri Becquerel discovered mineral radioactivity. He was the first to detect the natural radiation from uranium salts. Scientists noted that gamma radiation—a type of ray emanating from some radioactive minerals—was very similar to that of X-rays. Both are forms of energy carried by photons—particles of electromagnetic radiation such as light or radio waves. The newly discovered mineral radiation showed a higher level of energy compared to X-rays.

Marie Curie was inspired by Becquerel's discovery and isolated radium in 1902. The blue light emitted from the element fascinated French citizens. The light suggested to some that radium might have medical powers. Physicians in France and around the world were also intrigued by the phenomenon and some began to experiment with various radium treatments. In 1907, two Parisian doctors acquired a tiny sample of the scarce radium salts and used it on a patient's skin to treat angioma, a rash-like disorder. Curie agreed that this treatment might also be a possible cure for skin cancer. Unfortunately, the early medical procedures were crude and often resulted in general tissue damage. Indeed, the radium salts sometimes caused, rather than cured, skin cancer.

Between 1900 and 1950, radioactive minerals declined in their medical significance while specialists gradually refined their ability to control the focus and intensity of X-radiation. With the advent of the cyclotron in the 1930s, researchers became capable of generating artificial isotopes, many of which were radioactive. Isotopes are atoms that have more or fewer neutrons than their parent element. The researchers found that many of these isotopes

Antoine-Henri Becquerel was the first to detect mineral radioactivity. He shared the Nobel Prize in physics of 1903 with Pierre and Marie Curie. (Courtesy of the National Library of Medicine)

were strongly radioactive and sometimes provided advantages over X-rays. For example, in the late 1950s, researchers discovered that radioactive cobalt could be used to generate a tight beam of gamma rays. Because the rays from cobalt 60 could penetrate through—but did not harm—the skin, equipment using this type of radioactivity became a dominant means of radiation treatment for cancer. While some progress was being made in X-ray technology, cobalt led a shift in attention back to mineral radiation. Soon many artificial isotopes were available to medical researchers and physicists. One of the products that quickly became prominent in medical diagnostics and treatment was radioactive iodine (iodine 131).

Physicians accelerated the advance of nuclear medicine when they began introducing radioactive iodine into a patient's body by mouth or injection as a means to help solve diagnostic problems with the thyroid gland. The technique was widely adopted when X-ray scans proved to be inadequate. Soft tissue areas—such as thyroid glands—are difficult to image with standard X-rays because these rays can yield ambiguous pictures.

The iodine is taken up by the cells of the thyroid gland and generates gamma-ray signals that produce high-resolution images of the gland. The results are relatively unambiguous because the iodine is not absorbed by any tissues of the body other than the thyroid gland. The procedure is also relatively safe because any excess iodine is quickly excreted in the urine.

The thyroid has played such an important role in the progress of nuclear medicine that a quick glance at its place in conventional medicine is warranted. The thyroid is a small gland at the base of the throat. It produces thyroxin, a hormone that is essential to growth. A shortage of iodine, the major component of thyroxin, leads to a swelling of the thyroid gland—the main symptom of a condition called goiter. Goiters caused by iodine shortage were fairly common in the 18th and 19th centuries. However, this condition is now rare in industrialized countries because modern dietary salt is supplemented with sodium iodide. At the present time, most goiters found in industrialized countries are a result of genetic malfunctions.

Health-care providers in ancient times recognized goiter as a serious disease and prescribed various remedies. Chinese physicians, as early as 1,000 years before the present era, treated the condition with teas brewed from seaweed or burnt sponges. Of course, they did not know that teas made from sea creatures contained traces of iodine and thus were a therapy for goiter. Since the treatments were often successful, word spread around the globe. In the early 1800s, a seaweed tea was used as an English folk remedy for goiter.

By about 1816, William Prout, an English country doctor, recognized the role of iodine in such treatments. In an effort to understand the medicinal qualities of sea vegetation, Dr. Prout analyzed seaweed tea and discovered the presence of iodine. Additional research convinced him that iodine ingestion could cure goiter. He prescribed doses of potassium iodide rather than relying on the questionable potency and purity of seaweed tea. Prominent London physicians adopted Prout's ideas around 1819 and the trend was reinforced by the successful treatments reported by French doctors. Unfortunately, the popularity of the iodide remedy also resulted in a tendency to overdose patients. Some physicians believed that if a small dose of potassium iodide was therapeutic, a larger dose would be better. Common practice led physicians to prescribe the compound in amounts more than 2,000 times the needed dosage. A possible consequence was a condition called iodism that was characterized by tremors and weight loss. By 1878, researchers determined that goiter could be controlled by prescribing very small amounts of iodine. The acceptance of this finding was slow, but by the 1890s the results of animal studies convinced health-care professionals that small doses were safer and better.

In a more modern setting, the basic health of the thyroid gland can be determined when small amounts of a radioactive iodine compound are injected into the body or swallowed in a capsule. After a short time, doctors can detect the amount of radioactivity present in the thyroid area. Since goiter causes the thyroid to enlarge, the swollen glandular tissue absorbs a larger quantity of the radioactive iodine than does normal tissue.

Though not medically related to goiter, cancer of the thyroid is always a possibility if the patient experiences significant swelling of the thyroid gland area. The presence of thyroid cancer—like that of goiter—can be diagnosed after introducing a radioactive isotope of iodine into the patient's body. A cancerous thyroid is diagnosed when a lump (a dark shadow made visible by the radioactive material) is seen on the photographic film.

The principal treatment for thyroid cancer is surgery, but radiation therapy is frequently employed as a follow-up procedure. Soon after surgery, the patient is injected with a stronger radioactive iodine compound than was used in the diagnostic tests. This material is intended to kill the scraps of cancerous tissue that might have escaped detection during the surgery.

In general, the use of radioiodine—which began after the 1960s—initiated the advances in nuclear medicine that occurred toward the end of the century. The discovery that detailed images of internal organs could be obtained by introducing radioactive materials into the body was vital to this progress. Scientists sought isotopes with periods of radioactivity that would allow time for administration and scanning but would not linger in the body after the completion of these functions. They also hoped to find radioactive materials—other than the allergy-producing iodine used to diagnose thyroid conditions—that would exhibit affinities for particular organs or organ systems.

For example, radioactive isotopes of the elements thallium and technetium were found to be particularly good for imaging coronary arteries, the vessels that supply blood to the heart muscle. There are now over 40 different artificial isotopes available to physicians and biomedical researchers. Some are used as general sources of gamma radiation to combat cancer. Others, like iodine, perform special roles because of affinities to particular organs or their ability to act as "tracers" by attaching to molecules that have particular bodily functions.

New Cancer Treatments

After 1960, significant strides were made in the precision of cancer-killing radiation therapy. These new developments included the use of proton beams in place of the standard gamma radiation. The proton ray carries a positive electrical charge while gamma rays and X-rays are electrically neutral. Because of this positive charge, the amount of energy given off by the ray and the depth to which it penetrates can be more carefully controlled by magnetic coils that serve as a lens through which the proton beams are focused. The protons can be highly concentrated in the target area and react strongly with nearby atoms. If these atoms are part of a cancer cell, the reaction can damage the cell and ultimately kill it. By using the more precise proton beam, the destructive effect on non-cancerous tissue is restricted to a smaller area. Indeed, the beam does not harm the healthy tissue located a few millimeters from the target.

The use of intersecting gamma rays is another affective method of killing cancer cells. In this technique, called a gamma knife, two or three relatively low-energy gamma rays are aimed to intersect at a precise area of cancerous tissue. When the target is bombarded by the combined radioactive beams, the cancer-killing effect is amplified. This method is particularly useful in treating brain tumors where damage to the surrounding tissue must be minimized.

As the number of medically useful isotopes increased, the need for economical methods for separating isotopes from their parent element became intense. The problem of separation stems from the fact that isotopes have the same chemical characteristics as the parent element. The only distinguishing feature is a slight difference in weight. The problem is compounded by the fact that the amounts of the isotope relative to the amounts of the parent element tend to be small. This is true of natural isotopes because in nature, the isotope decays faster than the parent element—sometimes much faster. The relative proportions are similar for artificial isotopes because when the parent is bombarded by neutrons, only a relatively small number actually absorb one of the neutrons into their nuclei.

Isotope separation was a significant problem in the early days of nuclear energy research. At that time, large, expensive facilities and huge, costly apparatus were needed to separate a lighter, more radioactive, uranium isotope from the heavier uranium parent element. The more highly radioactive isotope was necessary to sustain a nuclear chain reaction.

Early attempts at separation used uranium hexafluoride, a highly corrosive gas, in the thermal diffusion system that used glass cylinders with chilled walls and heated center areas so that the lighter isotope would tend to move upward while the heavier tended to move downward in the cylinder. In this system some of the lighter isotopes could be skimmed off at the top of the column. The captured gas was repeatedly reprocessed by thermal diffusion to obtain a higher concentration of uranium 235. A somewhat more efficient system used corrosion-resistant filters. A slight pressure was used to force some gas molecules through the filter. A few more of the lighter molecules went through than the heavier molecules.

John Lawrence, brother to Ernest Lawrence, helped direct the efforts to develop an economical method for the separation of radioactive isotopes that would be useful in medicine. (Courtesy of the National Library of Medicine)

Later, scientists sought to discover a still more efficient method of obtaining the isotope separation by using large, high-speed centrifuge machines. In this case, the gaseous mixture is injected into resistant tubes and spun so rapidly that the slightly heavier U-238 molecules sink to the bottom. The lighter, more radioactive isotopic molecules rise to the top and are captured. Unfortunately, this procedure is also inefficient. Over a period of several months, 30,000 centrifuge machines—working full time—could produce only a few kilograms of refined uranium. In any case, when a reasonable concentration was reached, the gas was subjected to chemical treatments to remove the fluoride. The final product— enriched, metal ingots containing a relatively high proportion of uranium 235—could be used to sustain a nuclear chain reaction in a nuclear power plant.

Scientists still continued to seek more efficient, cost-saving methods of isotope separation for nuclear energy application. In the 1980s, a new process called laser isotope separation (LIS) proved to be an improvement. LIS was developed initially at the research facilities managed by the University of California under the guidance of John Lawrence (the brother of Ernest Lawrence, the inventor of the cyclotron). Advanced development work was transferred to the Lawrence Livermore National Laboratory managed by the University.

The process—which requires much smaller and less expensive equipment than the earlier methods—involves heating a chemical element until it vaporizes and then directing the vapor flow into a laser beam. Since all elements (and their isotopes) absorb some light frequencies and reflect others, the laser beam—a strong light source—is carefully tuned to provide the exact absorption frequency of the isotope to be separated. This allows the parent element to pass through the beam without being changed. As the vaporous isotope passes through the laser beam, the energy of the laser drives a negatively charged electron from each targeted isotopic atom and those atoms acquire a positive charge. The positively charged atoms are then drawn to a negatively charged col-

The site of the Lawrence Livermore National Laboratory, where staff personnel work on many of the practical applications of nuclear energy, including the separation of medically useful isotopes. (Courtesy of the U.S. Department of Energy)

lector plate. After being collected, they are stored in special containers until used.

Although LIS was originally intended primarily for uranium isotopes, the technique will work with other elements. Therefore, radioactive isotopes of medically effective elements—those used for diagnostic and surgical procedures—can be produced more easily and cheaply. Indeed, the isotope calcium 43, used for detecting problems in the arteries that feed the heart, can be separated from the parent element at an operating cost of a few dollars per milligram. Older methods, such as the use of a centrifuge, could cost up to $400 per milligram.

LIS requires a high level of technical ability. Its use should be limited to qualified and approved scientists who are involved in producing isotopes for medical procedures or peaceful applications of atomic energy. Unfortunately, the equipment can also be used to produce weapons-grade fissionable material. The comparatively compact equipment is small enough to be disguised or hidden and could be undetected by international weapons inspectors.

Imaging

Sooner or later someone was bound to consider whether computers could help improve the quality of medical imaging. The question was answered by the development of tomography. This method allows the virtual examination of a specific organ by viewing 3D computer images processed from a large series of two-dimensional X-rays. The technique begins with scanning multiple X-ray pictures of successive layers (called slices) of a specific organ. As these the layers are scanned, the angle of scanning is gradually changed in order to provide highly detailed images. The raw images gathered in this way do not make a coherent picture. In order to obtain a diagnostic tool, the component images must be processed by a computer using a complicated method called a transform program. The program rearranges the component parts to form a readable picture of the shape and structure of the target organ. The result is a CT (computerized tomography) scan, commonly called a CAT (computerized axial tomography) scan. The computerized images of layered cross sections of the body are one of the most sophisticated diagnostic tools provided by modern X-ray technology.

The next step in refining this diagnostic tool was to combine the techniques of isotopic imaging and tomography. The general term for this combination is positron emission tomography, or PET scans. This type of imaging allows physicians to detect how a target organ is functioning. In order to reach the full

An early version of CT or computerized tomography. In this device, the body was maintained in an upright posture. (Courtesy of the National Library of Medicine and the World Health Organization)

potential of PET, new work was needed to identify radioactive isotopes and organic molecules with special affinities for specific organ systems. Biochemists soon identified the effective isotopes and the organic molecules that could transport isotopes best suited for this function. Thus, the radioactive material could be carried to the target and generate signals that would be translated into images. The images showed how the normal and abnormal organ tissue utilized the isotopic material.

Glucose molecules are an example of an effective isotope carrier. Research had shown that glucose (a sugar compound made up of carbon, oxygen, and hydrogen) has a natural affinity for muscle cells. Chemists are able to replace the original carbon atoms with the isotopic carbon. The radioactive glucose, introduced into the body by ingestion, is absorbed by muscle cells. The images generated by the radioactive material show the rate of absorption and are used to determine the health of the muscle.

To facilitate a difficult diagnosis, physicians often combine X-ray and isotope imaging in a procedure called CT/PET—computerized tomography/positron emission tomography. In a normal decay sequence, all isotopes emit some positrons—the positively charged counterparts of electrons. Each positron quickly collides with a nearby electron. The impact generates two photons—the particles that carry light energy. Like X-rays, these gamma rays can penetrate tissue and generate a readable image. The resulting gamma energy is detected by the same device that registers the energy from X-rays. The practice of simultaneously scanning both types of images produces pictures that are far more detailed than the record generated by a single technique.

Magnetic resonance imaging (MRI) is an even more sophisticated diagnostic technique and requires a complicated piece of scanning equipment. Magnetic resonance imaging uses electromagnets of astonishing power. Workers are required to remove magnetically sensitive objects before entering the test facility and people with pacemakers are barred from entering the unit. The typical MRI magnetism has the tremendous strength of about 60,000 times the Earth's own magnetic field. The magnet is

This MRI machine at the University of Utah has a main magnet with a strength of 3 Tesla and is among the most powerful in use. (Courtesy of M. H. Huntsman, Department of Radiology)

generated by a coil of superconducting wire that is super-cooled to –452.4 degrees F (–270 degrees Celsius) by liquid helium. The supercooling makes the coil a *superconductor* so that it offers no resistance to electric current. Therefore, after it has been activated, the electromagnetic coil requires no further input of electrical current and can generate the strong magnetic field.

MRI technique is based on the fact that the *nucleus* of every hydrogen atom is magnetic and will line up in an orderly fashion when exposed to a strong magnetic field. The MRI's magnetic field emanates from electromagnetic coils that surround the patient's body. The orderly alignment of the hydrogen nuclei is shifted when a much less powerful radio frequency is directed at the patient's body. The radio frequency used in MRI scans pulses from coils positioned between the patient and the strong electromagnetic coils. The timing of the radio frequency is controlled by a computer, which also directs the scanning sequence of the target organs. When the radio frequency is turned off, the hydrogen nuclei revert to their previous alignment. Signals sent by the repositioning nuclei are detected and processed by the computer, which then generates a readable image of the physical condition of the organ being scanned.

Researchers claim that brain images generated by MRI are so revealing that they can observe changes in a patient's thought patterns. Indeed, if the patient is shown emotion-arousing photographs—such as a beautiful baby or a devastating war scene—changes will appear in the MRI scan. Some bioethicists are concerned that such brain scans could be used to invade an individual's privacy. Another ethical issue arises from the relatively high cost of MRI equipment and the operational costs: Not all disease victims have access to the most advanced systems.

9

Recovery from the Era of Bomb Making

There are two aspects in the efforts of the federal government to reduce the exposure of citizens to nuclear hazards. One aspect is the continuing program aimed at limiting the production of nuclear weapons. This effort is international in scope and involves U.S. participation in the functions of the United Nations as well as direct negotiations with other countries.

The second aspect is localized within the borders of the United States. It covers the activities of many government bodies such as the Department of Energy, the Department of Defense, and the Environmental Protection Agency to manage the nuclear materials that are the by-products of weapon production.

The New Era of Arms Control

After an initial failure, a new arms control unit called the International Atomic Energy Agency was formed by the United Nations in July 1957. The general strategy of the U.N. negotiators began to change at this time. Rather than seeking a broad agreement, the effort was directed toward more modest goals. International officials believed that agreement would be easier on smaller issues. Once these were resolved, it might be possible to assemble them in a more comprehensive arrangement.

The new strategy worked, and a partial ban on tests in the atmosphere was accomplished in August 1963 and ratified by about 70 countries in October of that year. This success was followed by the Treaty of Tlatelolco in February 1967. This treaty prohibited the possession of any nuclear weapons by the nations of Latin America. Prohibitions on nuclear testing in space, on the seafloor, and in Antarctica followed in succession. However, the ban on atmospheric testing of nuclear devices served mainly to promote underground tests as an alternative. For example, in the United States, 360 underground detonations were initiated between 1963 and 1979. In the Soviet Union, there were 162 such detonations.

New Departures

The mixed outcomes of the treaties negotiated under U.N. supervision influenced the responses of the negotiators representing the United States and the Soviet Union. In the early 1970s moves began to work toward direct agreements—treaties that would commit the two large countries on matters that did not require the participation of others.

The first of these so-called bilateral agreements was ratified under the leadership of President Richard Nixon in October 1972. The treaty called for restrictions in the production and deployment of defensive systems called antiballistic missile systems. The common name for this agreement was the Strategic Arms Limitation Treaty on Anti-Ballistic Missiles, or SALT ABM.

Meanwhile, efforts to stop underground tests were under way. In July 1974 under President Gerald Ford, an agreement called the Threshold Test Ban Treaty was signed. This agreement limited the size of underground nuclear explosions.

Test area in Nevada where both surface and underground test detonations of atomic bombs were carried out. (Courtesy of the U.S. National Archives and Records Administration)

A very broad arms limitation agreement was signed in June 1979 at the direction of President Jimmy Carter. This treaty, called SALT II, put upper limits on the number and size of ballistic missiles.

Back to the United Nations

The military capabilities of the Soviet Union began to decline in the 1980s, and the union fell apart in 1991 when areas within the union, such as the Ukraine, declared their independence. The principal remnant of the former Soviet Union was Russia. It declared itself an independent republic in 1992.

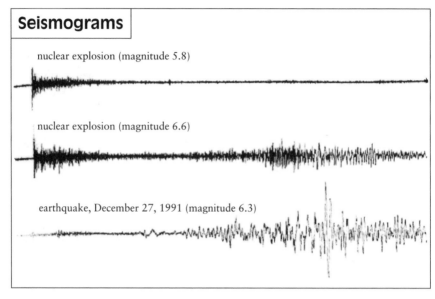

Seismograms

nuclear explosion (magnitude 5.8)

nuclear explosion (magnitude 6.6)

earthquake, December 27, 1991 (magnitude 6.3)

The sudden onset of vibration in the seismographic record provides a distinctive signature for a nuclear detonation compared to the record from a natural earthquake.

The leaders of the new Russia made overtures to the leaders of the United States to revitalize the discussions on disarmament within the setting of the United Nations. These moves led to the draft formulation of an agreement called the Comprehensive Test Ban Treaty (CTBT) in January 1994.

While these negotiations were going on, persistent disagreements centered on monitoring and enforcement. Each side was reluctant to trust the other to refrain from test detonations. Both felt a need to be able to detect any violation of the agreements as written. In the words of the negotiators, they wanted to be able to verify compliance.

In the years just before 1994, the main device for monitoring was an ordinary seismograph, originally designed to detect earthquakes. These machines did their original job well but were regarded as too unreliable and subject to errors for nuclear test detection. The weaknesses in detection led the American negotiators to seek on-site inspections, so if an ambiguous event was recorded by a seismograph, an international team would be able to go to the suspected site and do followup tests with instruments such as Geiger counters. The Russians would not agree to let such teams enter their country.

The blockage was resolved by turning to science and technology: Means to detect even very low-powered nuclear detonations from great distances without any mistakes would be developed.

Significant improvements were made to seismographs. These new machines were dedicated exclusively to the detection of nuclear events. Installations were built for these devices at stations around the world, and they were connected by a communication network that included computer processing of the seismic signals.

Similarly, stations were built to hold other kinds of detectors. Networks of sensors for radioactivity, airborne sound, and waterborne sound were put in place. If intensive analysis of the findings from all the detector systems still yield ambiguous results, on-site inspections are permitted. Both scientists and political negotiators, however, believe such a scenario to be extremely unlikely, making on-site inspections unlikely as well.

The principal parties to the CTBT agreement are the United States, Russia, the United Kingdom, France, and China. However, since it was put together within the United Nations, the signers include more than 150 nations. A small number of nations persist in testing nuclear devices for their own political reasons. Both India and Pakistan conducted underground bomb tests in 1998. Such explosions are regarded as against the general interests of humanity by the vast majority of political leaders around the world.

PLUTONIUM PRODUCTION AND REPROCESSING

During World War II and some 40 years of cold war, government officials were relatively unconcerned with the prospects that weapons production would contaminate the environment. All such matters were secondary to the production of enough weapons to restrain the hands of any nuclear opponent.

From late 1943 until 1988, the main source of plutonium for weapons was the Hanford facility in southeastern Washington State. Another installation on the Savannah River spanning the border between South Carolina and Georgia was where much of the plutonium was refined to the purity needed for weapons use. Along the Savannah was also a so-called breeder reactor that operated to produce more plutonium than it consumed as fuel. As a result, the area is contaminated by nuclear waste. Fissionable materials were also concentrated at Oak Ridge, Tennessee, the site of another breeder reactor on the nearby Clinch River. Its environment is also contaminated. Finally, Los Alamos in New Mexico and the Rocky Flats Arsenal in Colorado have similar problems because weapons were assembled at both, and finished weapons and large amounts of both uranium and plutonium are now stored there.

Hanford does not have the highest concentration of total contamination, but it provides the clearest picture of the total problem. Hanford is the most geographically extensive nuclear production site. It occupies 560 square miles (approximately 1,455 sq km) of territory. A major river, the Columbia, flows through one section of the site and along its eastern boundary. A total of nine reactors using uranium fuel to produce plutonium were built there between 1943 and 1963. During the work-life of these reactors, they produced a total of more than 220,000 pounds (100,000 kg) of plutonium metal. Each kilogram, just over two pounds, of plutonium production generated 340 gallons (about 1,310 l) of high-level waste and 55,000 gallons (about 210,000 l) of low-level waste, and used a total of 2.5 million gallons (9.5 million l) of coolant water.

Scattered over the site are 1,700 waste deposits—some in the form of single- or double-walled holding tanks for high-level liquid wastes. The storage tanks are typically about 75 feet (around 22.5 m) in diameter. The high-level liquid wastes come from plutonium separation, which entails dissolving depleted uranium fuel rods in nitric acid. These fuel rods, when depleted, contain the plutonium that has been formed by the neutronic bombardment of the uranium. The two metals, uranium and plutonium, form soluble nitrates and can be extracted from the solution by relatively simple chemical steps. The residue of nitric acid is then neutralized by the addition of caustic soda. The level of inherent radioactivity in this residue is somewhat suppressed by the further addition of sodium ferrocyanide and sodium titanate. These two chemicals force the radioactive by-product cesium 137 out of the solution but add

The Savannah River Plant was constructed primarily to refine the plutonium produced in their local reactor and elsewhere. (Courtesy of the U.S. Department of Energy)

significant amounts of carbon-containing compounds to the slurry. The result is a kind of sludge in which continuing chemical transformations are fostered by the warmth and energy generated by the radioactivity.

This sludge has been deposited in the waste storage tanks over the years. Some of the tanks—particularly those with single walls—leak fluids into the ground. Moreover, the chemical reactions that take place in the tanks produce hydrogen gas and some nitrous oxide, a highly flammable combination. This gas can be vented to the open air, but if the ventilation system fails, it could accumulate to dangerous levels.

The present plan is to dilute the sludge and run it through a screening system that will concentrate the high-level waste so that incorporating it into melted glass will be efficient. When the glass solidifies, it is impervious to water and resists all forms of weathering. The radioactive material cannot escape. The low-level waste separated from the high level-waste will be mixed with a cementlike product that will harden into a solid that can be buried in relatively shallow trenches.

In areas where the soil has been contaminated by leaks or misdirected dumping, officials are considering a technique for converting the soil into glass while the soil remains in place. For areas as large as 100 feet (30 m) in diameter, conversion might be achieved by placing high-capacity electrodes deep in the ground and generating heat by conducting high-voltage electric current through the soil.

The Hanford site is also highly polluted by chemicals other than radioactive compounds. For example, many carbon-based compounds have been dumped into ditches or ponds. Contractors have proposed using microbes to consume these chemicals, but tests indicate that such a process is extremely slow unless the microbes have been genetically engineered to be more efficient.

Altogether, there are 177 million gallons (about 673 million l) of high-level waste in the storage tanks at the Hanford site.

The best estimates suggest that the total cleanup of tanks, soils, and waterways will require 30 years to complete at a cost of perhaps as much as $50 billion. It seems likely that the time and cost of remediation of the other major sites will be less because they are more compact and plutonium was produced in lesser amounts in places other than Hanford.

SURPLUS WEAPONS

During the early stages of the cold war, hundreds of alternative weapons designs were invented. Different designs were needed for the bombs carried by aircraft and the warheads attached to

Technicians at the Pantex industrial complex worked under contract first to ensure that atomic weapons were maintained in good condition and later to disassemble retired weapons. (Courtesy of the U.S. Department of Energy)

ballistic missiles. Very small warheads were needed for artillery rounds. Some nuclear weapons were so small and light that they could be fired by an artillery piece manned by just two soldiers. However, by the end of the cold war in the late 1980s, the number of distinct designs had been reduced to just nine. Most of the fissionable material in most of these warheads is plutonium.

It is not possible to know how many warheads were in existence at the height of the cold war. The number may have been as high as 40,000 in the United States alone. At the end of the cold war, there were only 20,000 nuclear bombs in the 1990 U.S. military inventory of weapons. Reports indicate that the number was down to 16,000 by 1992. Projections for the future specified that there were only 5,000 in condition for immediate use in 2003, with another 5,000 in storage for replacements, if needed.

One of the major locations for the disassembly of nuclear warheads is the Pantex plant near Amarillo, Texas. At one time, the plant was busy putting nuclear weapons together; now it is in the business of taking the bombs apart. It is not an easy task. Some of the warhead materials and the bombs' complicated machinery have deteriorated over time. The immediate goal is to take apart about 1,400 warheads a year at the plant. The total quantity of plutonium taken out of bombs and prepare for storage or recycling will be at least 26 tons (26,000 kg).

10
Advances in Nuclear Power Generation

There were 104 nuclear power plants operating in the United States in 2005; these plants provide about 20 percent of the country's electric power each year. The actual output of these plants has increased each year because of upgrades in equipment and procedures. However, the relative contribution has remained constant because the other sources of power generation have increased along with population and industrial expansion.

There have been no new nuclear plants licensed for construction since the accident at the Three Mile Island power plant in late 1979. A few plants were authorized for construction in prior years and some of these were not completed until the mid-1990s. For example, the Watts Bar power plant in Tennessee was approved for construction in 1972 but did not begin to produce electricity until 1996.

Need for electric power is projected to continue to increase. Based on recent opinion surveys, about half the people in the United States would welcome additional nuclear power plants as the best way to meet the growing need. Nuclear plants do not contribute to climate change and air pollution—so even some strict environmentalists are not strongly opposed to nuclear energy initiatives. Provisions for plant safety have improved greatly since 1980, both with regard to equipment design and with regard to operator training and skill levels. However, other concerns remain and there are some quite intractable problems. Among them is the problem of nuclear waste.

Low-Level Nuclear Waste

Government authorities concerned with waste management base some of their decisions on the distinction between so-called low-level and high-level waste. This bureaucratic distinction is, in turn, based on the source of the waste. High-level waste is defined as waste that comes from the production of atomic weapons and from the depleted fuel rods used in nuclear power plants. Low-level waste is, essentially, everything else that might be radioactive. Materials include contaminated clothing, chemical solvents, building materials, tools and construction equipment, and even paper products.

Environmentalists and public health specialists assert that a better gauge for risk analysis would be the magnitude of radioactivity and the time required for its decline due to natural decay. Indeed, investigators have shown that some materials classified as low-level waste had higher levels of radiation than did by-products of the manufacture of nuclear weapons. One reasonable conclusion might be that the disposal of low-level waste should be given the same degree of scrutiny as is given to the methods of storage for high-level waste. Such has rarely been the case.

Low-Level Waste Sites

While the federal government has always had a clear responsibility for the waste generated from the use of nuclear materials by the armed services, legislation passed in the 1950s and later gave the separate states the job of handling the waste from other sources. The states, in turn, sought to engage private contractors to do the work.

For example, in the early 1950s, some states contracted to have their low-level waste treated like ordinary trash to be dumped in the ocean. This action generated such strong objections from the voters that it was soon dropped.

The next step for the states was to consider landfills as an option. Officials recognized that practices used for general garbage would not be satisfactory of nuclear waste—so special areas were designated to be used exclusively for radioactive materials.

Some state officials, eager to encourage the development of nuclear industry, sought certification of their designated sites by federal authorities. This required geological surveys of prospective sites and detailed plans for material handling operations. Since the 1960s, seven disposal sites have been licensed by the Nuclear Regulatory Commission. Three remained in operation in 2005.

Starting in 1962, the first commercial site opened in Beatty, Nevada, near the Atomic Test Area and Nellis Air Force Base. Sites at Richland, Washington (adjacent to the Hanford plutonium production facility); West Valley, New York; Maxey Flats, Kentucky; Sheffield, Illinois; and Barnwell, South Carolina (next to the Savannah River Nuclear Facility) opened in the years between 1963 and 1971. The most recent establishment was opened in Clive, Utah (near former uranium mining operations), in 1998. (The Richmond, Barnwell, and Clive sites are the ones still open in 2005.)

The past 43 years have been a learning period for federal and state officials and for the contractor personnel. In general, the story is one of unfounded optimism about containment. The principal reason for site closure has been leakage of radioactive materials into the water supplies of the surrounding territories. Contractors typically dug wide trenches into which the radioactive materials were placed (sometimes in cardboard boxes). After placement, soil was piled back so that the trench was filled in and a hump of soil was formed. Shortly, after a few rainstorms, the hump would collapse as dirt trickled into the gaps between storage containers in the trench. A shallow ditch would form that would hold standing water. The water would drain down from the ditch and dissolve some radioactive chemicals. Then the water would migrate into the ground water zones that fed wells. When radioactivity appeared in drinking water, local residents complained. Such was the general pattern of events in New York, Kentucky, and Illinois.

The enterprise in Nevada did not suffer from dispersal of radioactive materials in the groundwater because the area has little rainfall. The operation broke down for other reasons. Specifically, in 1990, federal and state officials were informed that workers at the site had removed contaminated machinery, tools and construction equipment. For example, a radioactive cement mixer was taken from the site.

Questions were raised about the quality of management supervision and new rules were levied to help ensure the safety of workers and local citizens. Conditions for continued use of the site deteriorated and finally the contractor was paid to shut down the facility. No new material was accepted after 1992 and the site was completely closed in 1994.

Probably the main lesson learned from the site failures was that handling even low-level nuclear waste was much more challenging and expensive than any ordinary landfill operation. Living near large amounts of municipal waste might be unpleasant, but living near a radioactive disposal site could be mortally dangerous.

The disposal situation is likely to become worse before it gets better. For example, in 2005, the Barnwell installation was reaching its maximum capacity and state officials were resisting the prospect of additional imports of radioactive material from the other states in the region.

Short-term projections suggest that most of the newly generated nuclear waste will end up at the site in Utah. This trend, which is already under way, will put increasing strain on transport arrangements. Transport methods have been refined over the past 50 years so that most material is packaged so that containment will not be lost even in a violent mishap. However, the new techniques continue to add to the costs of dealing with low-level waste.

High-Level Nuclear Waste

Depleted fuel rods from nuclear power plants are the main source of nonmilitary high-level radioactive waste material. Studies and analyses carried out by scientists in every country that has nuclear power plants all concur that the only realistic option is deep underground storage of depleted fuel rods. However, in 2005, there is no geological repository for these fuel rods in the United States. The fuel rods are now mainly stored in specially designed water tanks on the power plant sites. Storage capacity is running short—particularly in the face of some plants being closed down because of old age. When a plant closes down, all its fuel must go into storage. This process, called decommissioning, has already begun and is only being postponed by arbitrarily extending the licenses of some old plants.

In 1982, Congress passed a law that promised that government-controlled, off-site repository facilities would be available in 1998 at the latest. By 2005, power plant owners were threatening legal actions against the Department of Energy for failure to comply with this law.

Possible locations for a large underground facility were being considered as early as the late 1970s, and the Yucca Mountain site in Nevada headed the list from the beginning. This location had an extensive history in the early atomic age.

Yucca Ridge in Nevada appears to be uninhabited. (Courtesy of the U.S. Department of Energy)

The area is very sparsely populated and has low annual rainfall amounts. In the 1960s and 1970s, the general area was used to test nuclear weapons. Before the Strategic Arms Limitation Treaty of 1979, almost 900 atomic explosions were set off in the Nevada desert—the last 800 of them underground detonations.

In 1978, the Department of Energy initiated a scientific review of the geological characteristics of the site. In particular, officials needed an analysis of the likely frequency of earthquakes in the area. In 1987, preliminary geological surveys, combined with strong political considerations, led Congress to designate the Yucca Mountain site as the only site to be given further attention. This action reversed a long-standing commitment to the idea that at least three candidate sites would be reviewed before any final determination would be made. Exploratory tunneling into the Yucca Mountain ridge system began in 1994.

By 2004, it was clear that the majority of the voters in Nevada did not want a nuclear waste repository in their state, but it was also clear that, from a national perspective, there was really no alternative. State officials attempted to have the courts rule that the decision to use the Yucca Mountain site was unconstitutional. The courts did rule that the repository must be designed to withhold nuclear contaminants for more than 10,000 years, but they threw out the constitutional issue.

In the meantime, the best scientific advice from domestic sources and from analyses done by scientists from other countries was to move ahead slowly. The scientists found no good reason why temporary storage in water tanks or in specially designed storage depots aboveground could not be used for at least another 10 years.

Advances in technology could allay parts of the problem during that span. Scientists and engineers have already developed some novel alternatives to deep burial. One is vitrification. This means mixing nuclear material with sand or clay and then heating the mixture to the melting point of the sand or heating the clay to form a ceramic. Most vitrification programs have been aimed at the disposal of radioactive liquids or the treatment of contaminated soils. Some of the plans for the deep underground storage already include the use of vitrification and double enclosure in a stainless steel shell. While the composite of glass and high-level nuclear material is still radioactive, vitrification helps in handling and transporting such materials and reduces the likelihood that the nuclear materials could be used in an illegal way.

Vitrification was pioneered by European scientists and engineers. So was recycling of nuclear fuel, another option that would reduce the need to store waste. Indeed, at present, recycling is regarded as an essential economy in the operation of nuclear power plants in France and Germany.

When a fuel rod is "expended," over 90 percent of the radioactivity remains. Much of this remainder is in the form of uranium 238 that does not support the chain reaction needed for power plant operations. Some of the material is in the form of fission by-products such as strontium. Some of it is plutonium—which does have power generation capabilities.

In order to be used again as fuel, the uranium must be re-enriched. The rods are broken up and the material is dissolved in acid. The different metals can be separated from one another by chemical means. The fission by-products can be stored separately and the uranium can be made into uranium hexafluoride and re-enriched. The enriched uranium and the plutonium are neutralized chemically and then oxidized, ground into a powder, and blended together. The powder is formed into pellets and the pellets are inserted into the steel tubes that become new fuel rods. The process is quite costly and hazardous.

This photo shows a section of the housing for the drill used in boring tunnels into the Yucca mountain. (Courtesy of the U.S. Department of Energy)

Most recycling is done in France. Scientists and engineers at the U.S. Department of Energy have been monitoring the French recycling program but by 2005 had not determined that the procedure would fit in well with American nuclear policies.

The option with the most far-reaching potential is transmutation. When Ernest Rutherford transmuted nitrogen into oxygen in 1905, he was warned not to use the term *transmutation* because of its connection with alchemists and charlatans. A century later, it is still not technically or economically feasible to transmute lead into gold but some elements can be transmuted by bombardment with neutrons. Indeed, some of the most dangerous elements in radioactive waste are candidates for transmutation by neutron bombardment.

Spallation Research

Spallation is a technique for generating streams of neutrons. The neutron streams are used to help analyze materials in fine detail. For example, neutrons can reveal the relative location of single atoms in complex molecules.

Neutron streams have been available to researchers for many years from the natural decay of uranium in nuclear reactors. Neutrons are the particles that generate the chain reaction that releases energy in nuclear power generation. However, the neutrons that come from uranium do not readily form a beam. As they emerge from the nucleus of a uranium atom, their movements are random. Some of these free neutrons can be channeled through special chambers built into the atomic pile but the number of neutrons that can be so directed is relatively small. Scientists interested in the detailed structure of materials, such as crystals and ceramic composites, wanted dense neutron streams that would generate high-resolution images.

Neutrons, like other subatomic particles, vibrate. Their vibration wavelength is very small. This wavelength is as small, or smaller, than the distance between atoms in a molecule. That characteristic is what allows neutrons to "see" such small details. Consequently, the motivation to produce more neutrons in beam formation was strong and a variety of techniques were explored. The technique that worked best was spallation. Specifically, a high-energy beam of protons is directed at a target made of a heavy metal such as mercury. When the protons strike the mercury atoms, they sometimes knock out a neutron. If enough protons are used, one microsecond's pulse of protons will dislodge thousands of neutrons in the form of a particle shower. Some of the neutrons can be brought together to form a stream because neutrons are sensitive to magnetic fields even though they do not carry an electrical charge. Magnets can be used to gently focus the burst of neutrons.

Once in a cluster and moving in the same direction, the neutrons need to be decelerated so that they can react with the material being analyzed. If the neutrons are moving too fast, they will simply pass through the sample. The most common speed retardant is water, so the neutrons are shunted through a water bath.

The most advanced facility for the generation of slow neutron beams is being constructed at the Oak Ridge National Laboratory in Tennessee. There, a team of nuclear scientists and engineers from the other National Laboratories is building a device that can be used to conduct several experiments simultaneously.

The operation of the spallation system will start with the injection of hydrogen atoms into an accelerator. When the hydrogen atoms are energized, they will be stripped of their electrons so that they become elemental protons. The protons will be directed onto the face of the mercury target and the dislodged neutrons will be collected and bunched at the backside of the target. After being slowed, sets of bunches will be directed into

The Neutron Spallation Laboratory is part of the Oak Ridge National Laboratory. (Courtesy of the Oak Ridge National Laboratory)

one of eight channels that will lead to the material to be analyzed. The neutron bunches will be organized in a sequence so that 60 bunches arrive at the material to be analyzed every second.

No government official is now suggesting that spallation is a possible remedy for high-level radioactive waste, but a steady supply of neutrons could alter the condition of such waste. For example, isotopes could be formed that would lose much of their radioactivity in a shorter time period.

Whether used on radioactive waste or not, this developmental project is another example of the physicists using their knowledge to support practical applications in areas such as biomedicine, structural engineering, and the design of components for electronic systems. For example, the next advance in recording motion pictures could well come from the studies of electronic materials that are scheduled at the Oak Ridge National Laboratory.

11

Advances in Nuclear Science

All scientists now recognize that atoms are composed of smaller particles. The atoms themselves are not the indivisible objects suggested by the ancient Greek philosophers. Indeed, atoms are divisible. One type of divisibility is illustrated by the hydrogen atom. This simple atom has one electron orbiting a nucleus with a single proton. The negatively charged electron and the positively charged proton balance each other, and the standard hydrogen atom is electrically neutral. However, certain electrical forces can separate the electron from its orbit around the nucleus. The electron becomes a free particle that can produce static electricity.

After the separation of the electron, the hydrogen atom consists of a nucleus with a single positively charged proton. It is called a positive *ion*. Other elements can form ions—positive or negative—when electrons are separated from or added to the atom.

Progress in the Late 20th Century

PARTICLE DETECTORS

Cosmic rays were discovered after the invention of a device that could detect the presence of invisible, energetic particles.

The first detectors were panels covered with phosphorescent material. A spark appeared when this material was struck by an invisible atomic particle. A better device called a cloud chamber was invented by the Scottish physicist Charles Wilson in 1895. At the time he created his detector, Wilson was working with J. J. Thomson at the Cavendish Laboratory at Cambridge University. Wilson's device was used by Thomson to help determine the weight of the invisible electron.

The principle of the cloud chamber is simple. One end of a glass container is removed and replaced by a metal sleeve fitted with a piston. The piston completely seals the airtight glass container. After warm, moist, dust-free air is introduced into the container, the piston is pulled back into the sleeve and the air expands into the newly created space. The air cools as it becomes less compressed but continues to hold all the moisture. Air that holds an abnormal amount of moisture is known as supersaturated. When an electricity charged particle enters the glass container through its walls, the particle's presence is

Tracks of bubbles are made by charged particles in the 72-inch cloud chamber. (Courtesy of the Lawrence Berkeley National Laboratory)

marked by the formation of a tiny droplet. When many charged particles enter the chamber, a cloud of droplets is formed inside the container. In a short time, the droplets of water will fall on a plate that can conduct electricity. This allows the total charge of the accumulated droplets to be measured.

In 1907, Hans Geiger invented a device that detects the presence of electrically charged particles as they pass by an array of fine wires. The signal emitted from the particles is strengthened by an electrical current that runs through the wires. (This method of strengthening a signal is also used in radio and television.) A speaker relays the strengthened signal as the sound of a click. A Geiger counter registers the flow-rate of the charged particles on a dial and by the speed of the clicks. The highly recognizable clicking sound is often used in TV and films to dramatize a situation in which nuclear material is nearby.

Over the years, the concept of Wilson's cloud chamber has been advanced. One such improvement led to the bubble chamber, invented in 1952 by the American physicist Donald Glaser. In this method, pure gases such as neon are chilled until they became liquid. The prepared liquids are placed in glass containers, and the vessels are warmed. The tightly sealed receptacles do not allow the heated liquid to expand, and the contents are kept under pressure. Such pressurized liquid cannot boil. However, if a charged particle enters the chamber, the particle will leave a trail of bubbles in its wake.

Another method of recording invisible electrically charged particles makes use of a clear gel made from a carbon-based material and silver iodide. The mixture is kept in a dark room and then placed in a lightproof container. When the mixture is exposed to radiation, the presence of any electrically charged particles will be indicated by black tracks visible in the gel. In this case, the path of the particle can be observed as its electrical charge converts the silver iodide into metallic silver. The method generates a record that will remain intact for hours or days.

Cosmic Rays

In the early 1900s, the German physicist Victor Hess was studying the natural radiation that comes from the surface of Earth. By the use of a cloud chamber, he determined that Earth's surface was weakly radioactive, giving off charged particles that could be detected. To gain more specific information, Hess ascended above Earth in a tethered balloon. He employed his cloud chamber to measure the decrease in radiation as he moved upward. The level of radioactivity declined in a regular manner until he was several hundred feet above Earth. Beyond this point, however, as he rose still higher, the intensity of the radiation began to increase again. This phenomenon seemed strange to Hess because the radiation came from above the balloon's gondola. At first, he thought the source might be the Sun, but the level of radiation remained constant after the Sun had set. Hess eventually concluded that most of the energetic particles were coming from outer space. He called them cosmic rays.

The actual source of these particles is still unknown. However, scientists now know that many of the particles in cosmic rays are extremely energetic protons; in fact, these protons are far more energetic than those produced by the best of today's particle accelerators. The earth's plants and animals do not develop radiation diseases from these protons because the particles of cosmic rays are few in number. In addition, Earth's atmosphere slows some and absorbs others.

The scarcity of cosmic rays has allowed little research on this type of particle. Nevertheless, this research gave physicists the idea that electrons, protons, and neutrons were not the only atomic particles in our universe. One eye-opening clue was the discovery of the positron in 1932. The American physicist Carl Anderson made his discovery on a mountaintop while using a Wilsonian cloud chamber to register cosmic rays.

A positron is an independent particle that has the very small mass of an electron but a positive electric charge. The nature of the positron did not agree with established theories on atomic structure. The implications taken from this irregularity were varied. Some scientists believed that the existence of the tiny positron might indicate the existence of particles with the larger mass of a proton but with a negative charge. An atom with a negatively charged nucleus orbited by a positively charged positron would have the opposite configuration from a normal atom. This phenomenon is referred to as an *anti-atom*. Indeed, the discovery generated the interesting idea that whole galaxies could be composed of antimatter.

Neutrinos

Another theory resulting from Anderson's discovery implied the existence of particles too rare or too short-lived to be easily detected during an analysis of cosmic rays. Such ideas were encouraged by the work of the German scientist Wolfgang Pauli, around the same time as Anderson's discoveries. Pauli calculated that when a neutron disintegrates into a proton and an electron, the mass of these two particles does not equal the mass of the original neutron. Pauli proposed that the missing mass belongs to a neutral particle that holds the protons together. A short time later, Enrico Fermi, who was working on the mathematics of neutron decay, gave the name "neutrino" to the missing neutral particle.

The neutrino is an elusive atomic particle with very little mass. It has no electrical charge and does not interact easily with other particles. The first demonstration of its actual existence was in 1953 at the Savannah River nuclear reactor in South Carolina. Physicists believed that the vast quantity of atomic particles generated by the reactor might include some of the elusive neutrinos. After a careful investigation, the researchers reported that a neutrino had reacted with another particle and generated a neutron and a positron. The positron then interacted with an electron and produced photons. The photons were detectable as a tiny flash of light.

In 1968, neutrinos from the Sun were observed by Raymond Davis using a large tank filled with pure carbon tetrachloride, a substance used in dry cleaning. The tank was made of stainless steel to block any local radioactivity, and it was set up deep underground to eliminate effects from cosmic rays. Light

The newest neutrino detector is being installed 0.6 mile (1,000 m) deep underground in the Kamioko mine in Japan. The steel outer shell will be immersed in a water tank to shield out cosmic rays. The inner tank is plastic and contains special oil that responds to energetic particles with a flash of light. (Courtesy of the Lawrence Berkeley National Laboratory)

detectors were used to record the tiny flashes from the photons produced by the neutrinos.

Modern facilities in Canada, central Europe, Cleveland, Ohio, and northern Minnesota follow the same general design but use purified water rather than carbon tetrachloride. The largest of the new detectors is in Japan. It is called the Super-Kamiokande and is located .6 miles (1,000 m) underground in an abandoned zinc mine. It contains 125 million gallons (475 million l) of distilled water and is lined with 13,000 photo detector tubes. A team of Japanese, American, and European physicists completed 500 days of observations in the spring of 1998. These observations provided strong evidence that the neutrino does have a small mass. Because neutrinos are so numerous, they probably make up most of the mass in the universe even though the individual particles are so very small.

Inside the Nucleus

Before and after World War II, the study of odd, exotic particles such as positrons and neutrinos inspired new theories about the origin of the universe. Physicists began to speculate about the existence of particles with energy levels far beyond those produced in nuclear reactors by controlled fission. They also hoped to determine the characteristics of the main components in normal, everyday matter and considered the possibility that protons and neutrons might be divisible. Indeed, scientists sought to discover and study all existing particles.

Between 1950 and 1970, many new accelerators were commissioned to investigate these ideas. Some of the machines were straight-line, or linear, such as the two-mile- (3.2-km-) long accelerator at Stanford University. However, most were circular, like the cyclotron developed at the University of California at Berkeley between 1930 and 1932 by Ernest Lawrence and his graduate student Stanley Livingston.

Lawrence's first cyclotrons were less than one foot (30 cm) in diameter. The world's most powerful machines are now about 18 miles (29 km) in diameter and have circumferences of about 28 miles (45 km).

The more violent the collision, the more likely that new and exotic particles will be generated by the crash.

With the advent of ever-larger accelerators, the devices to detect particles have also become larger and more elaborate. Scientists need these more complicated detectors to gain as much information as possible from each collision. Indeed, the rising costs of collisions have curtailed the number of experiments that can be performed.

To increase the knowledge gained from each event, several different types of detectors are placed around the collision site. Today, computers are programmed to sort the rare and interesting from the common and dull. Powerful computers can select important information from hundreds of events in millionths of a second and are standard equipment at every major accelerator installation.

The Particle Zoo

After World War II, the increase in the number of particle accelerators expanded the variety of identifiable particles. Many of these artificially generated particles may be the same as those that played significant roles when the first burst of energy formed the universe. Most have no function in present-day matter.

Among the natural particles are electrons, protons, and neutrons. In the 1930s, Pauli and Fermi proposed that the nuclei of all atoms larger than hydrogen were held together by the neutrino. Today, this function has been reassigned to the meson, and the neutrino is no longer regarded as an essential particle.

Today, electrons and *nucleons*—the term that refers to both protons and neutrons—are the crucial particles that make up ordinary atoms. In the mid-1950s, scientists began an attempt to determine the internal structure of protons. The newly built linear accelerator at Stanford University allowed high-energy collisions between electrons and protons. The mass of the particles resulting from these crashes and the change in direction and velocity of the electrons were recorded. By this time, electrons were known to be indivisible, but the data suggested that protons are composed of two or three smaller particles. Much of the Stanford research was conducted by Robert Hofstadter.

Hofstadter was born in New York City in 1915. He was an excellent student and received his undergraduate degree with honors from the City College of New York in 1935. Three years later, in 1938, Hofstadter was awarded both a master's and a doctorate in physics from Princeton University in New Jersey.

After a pair of postdoctoral fellowships, he accepted a position at the National Bureau of Standards in Washington, D.C. In late 1941, when the United States entered World War II, Hofstadter began working for the Norden Laboratory Corporation in New York. This company designed and built precision bomb sights for high-altitude strategic bombers.

After the war, Hofstadter returned to Princeton and worked on advanced techniques to detect high-energy particles. His work led to an invitation to join the faculty at Stanford University in Palo Alto, California. The Stanford Linear Accelerator was under construction when he arrived in 1950. His special training allowed him to design complex detectors to record the data from collisions between high-velocity electrons and protons. Although the accelerator was usable by 1953, designers modified and lengthened the machine until its completion in 1966. As early as the mid-1950s, many of Hofstadter's experiments indicated that the proton might be a composite particle.

During the postwar years, new accelerators were built at Cornell University in Ithaca, New York, and other locations. New particles continued to be discovered. Many of these particles were heavier than protons. Scientists observed that they behaved in an unusual but reoccuring manner when they collided with other particles in an accelerator. After careful investigation, physicists such as Murray Gell-Mann decided that *hadrons* might be composed of positively and negatively charged subparticles. These subparticles appeared to be normally arranged in groups of three. Gell-Mann assigned the word *quark* to the category of subparticles, the word *up* to the positive subparticles, and the word *down* to the negative subparticles. A positively charged proton contains two up subparticles and one down subparticle. The neutron, which has no electric charge, contains two downs and one up. Next, mathematical findings established that an up subparticle contains two-thirds the charge of a normal positive particle (a proton) and a down subparticle contains one-third the charge of a normal negative particle (an electron). In mathematical terms: $2/_3$ positive charge + $2/_3$ positive charge − $1/_3$ negative charge = $3/_3$ positive charge = a proton; $1/_3$ negative charge + $1/_3$ negative charge − $2/_3$ positive charge = 0 charge = a neutron.

Additional information from the collisions indicated that a third subparticle was needed to explain the strange heaviness detected in some hadrons. Not surprisingly, this subparticle is called the *strange quark.*

Quarks are held together in a hadron by a very peculiar particle called a *gluon.* The gluon is an example of the so-called strong force. The strong force is similar to the workings of a spring or rubber band, and its power becomes stronger when the quarks spread apart. In fact, the force is so strong that the quarks in protons and neutrons can never be permanently separated.

Information from newer, higher velocity accelerators revealed other, heavier particles. Three more quarks were discovered and named the *charmed quark,* the *bottom quark,* and the *top quark.* These names are all arbitrary and have no scientific meaning. They partly reflect the view that the nature of these particles has no parallel in ordinary experience.

The top quark is the largest and most recently discovered. In 1996, this subparticle was located by the sensitive detectors in the accelerator at Fermilab outside of Chicago. The most massive subparticles are generated by very high-energy collisions and have infinitesimally short lifespans. Hadrons containing top quarks have lifespans of less than a trillionth of a second and are therefore, remarkably difficult to detect. However, most physicists now believe that the powerful new accelerators have allowed them to identify all the basic subparticles found in hadrons.

The Missing Link

A simulated Higgs particle. While not yet detected, scientists think they know what its discovery might look like. This is a computer-generated image of the pattern expected from the particle detector. (Courtesy of CERN)

As yet, physicists do not fully understand how particles obtain their mass. They want to comprehend the great variations in weight found among subatomic particles. These variations range from particles with no mass—such as photons—to those of great mass—such as top quarks. In 1964, two very similar theories were put forth to help explain these peculiarities. The British physicist Peter W. Higgs offered one hypothesis, and the Belgium physicists Robert Brout and François

Englert proposed the other. Both theories state that these perceived inconsistencies can be explained by a force that is present but undetected in our universe. This force is now called a Higgs field.

If the particle that generates this field could be detected, it would help resolve many questions such as the extreme predominance of ordinary matter over antimatter. All the available evidence indicates that antimatter should be just as prevalent as normal matter, or at least that antimatter had the same chance to dominate the universe that normal matter had when the universe was first formed.

Progress at the Turn of the Century and Beyond

Most basic research in nuclear science is guided by the *Standard Model* theory. This theory provides a mathematical framework to integrate all that is known about electromagnetism and the forces that bind all particles. Interestingly, even though the properties of gravity are well understood, the Standard Model does not connect this information with the other physical forces. At the present time, theorists face a major challenge in integrating all the natural forces and the properties of the particles that carry such forces. Before this comprehensive unification can be achieved, a new generation of research instruments is needed to gain more information.

Particle accelerators, the principal equipment used for research on high-energy particles, have been employed by physicists since the 1930s. In the aftermath of World War II, the U.S. government financed the development of a wide range of such instruments. This equipment has been successively improved and made more powerful over the years.

Researchers are using the currently available accelerators to investigate high-energy particles, conduct chemical analysis, study the physical properties of matter, and investigate other important issues. When subatomic particles such as protons are energized in an accelerator, they can be focused to collide with fixed targets or with a stream of particles coming from the opposite direction. The fragments resulting from such collisions reveal the inner structure of the target materials or of the streaming particles themselves.

Today, there are about 20,000 particle accelerators in the world. The majority are concentrated in the highly industrialized areas of Europe, North America, and Asia. Most of these are relatively small, low-powered accelerators and are used in academic settings for student training or in commercial settings for the manufacture of medical and industrial products. Only a few dozen of the largest, most powerful of these instruments are used for basic research. These machines cost from millions of dollars for the smaller, less complicated models to hundreds of millions of dollars for the largest and most advanced.

If American physicists had had their way, the largest research accelerator in the world would have been located about 30 miles (48 km) southwest of Dallas, Texas. That site was to have been the home of the Superconducting Super Collider (SSC)—an instrument that would have been contained in a 54-mile (86-km wide), circular chamber. The town nearest the site is Boz, Texas, today a ghost town. The nearby town of Waxahachie, Texas (population 20,000) would have benefited most from the program. However, few benefits ever came to Waxahachie, because the SSC program was cancelled in 1993. In that year, the House of Representatives voted overwhelmingly to withhold further funding.

The construction of the SSC proved to have many technical and political problems. The main technical problem resulted from the huge, powerful magnets needed to propel the high-energy particles around the circular chamber. During the preliminary testing, the magnets were wound with superconducting

wires which had been super-
cooled by liquid helium. As
the strength of the magnets
was increased, the superconductivity of the wires was
weakened. The reason for this
glitch remained a mystery for
several years.

A more mundane but sur-
prisingly frustrating problem
was the discovery of fire ants.
The site of the tunnel was under
prairie land that was infec-
ted with these creatures. They
are very unpleasant because
they can inflict a painful and
annoying bite. During preliminary testing, workers found
that the ants also bit into
and ate the insulation on the
electrical wiring. An electrical

*The face plate of the large new
particle detector being installed at
CERN* (Courtesy of CERN)

short in the complicated wiring for the SSC could have been
disastrous.

The political problems concerning the project were evident in the conflicting statements about the project's goals.
Some saw a positive effect in providing a significant economic boost to that area of Texas. Others saw an excessive
drain on the federal budget. Some saw the project as a way
for the United States to remain at the forefront in scientific
research. A few saw the opportunity to attract international
scholars to participate in nuclear studies and then return
home to utilize their newfound information to compete with
American scientists. In any case, Congress finally rejected
the project after spending over two billion dollars in the
planning and initial construction of the site. An additional

Liquid helium is used to cool the superconducting wires that wrap the magnets at CERN (Courtesy of CERN)

half billion dollars was appropriated for an orderly shutdown of the project.

Many in the scientific community were devastated. Some no longer believed there would be a continuing effort to understand the physical universe. More optimistic scientists hoped that other research programs could continue the quest. In this case, the optimists were correct. Looking back to 1993, it is now reasonable to believe that the SSC would have been a strategic mistake on the part of nuclear scientists. The proposed size of the SSC was too large to support the research programs of the early 1990s but not large enough for the next major step—going beyond the study of *quarks.*

Recent Gains

International collaborations in particle physics have become more productive since the SSC project was discontinued. Today, CERN (the European Consortium for Nuclear Research) operates the most powerful accelerator in the world. This organization was created by the joint efforts of the industrialized countries of Europe. With a boost from the United Nations Educational, Scientific and Cultural Organization (UNESCO), 12 nations worked together in the early 1950s to initiate the nuclear research facility. There are now 20 member nations of CERN. The United States, Japan, India, Israel, Russia, and Turkey are "observer states" and 28 other countries are nonmember participants.

The headquarters of CERN is in the outskirts of Geneva, Switzerland, but the extensive grounds extend across the border into French territory. In fact, the tunnel that holds the accelerator is mainly in France. The tunnel is 16.2 miles (27 km) in circumference and 320 feet (100 m) below the ground. On average, 6,500 scientists from 80 different countries are in residence at the headquarters.

Under the general supervision of the Italian physicist Carlo Rubbia and the Dutch physicist Simon van der Meer, two new particles, the W boson and the Z boson, were discovered by CERN researchers in 1983. In the language of physicists, the word *boson* means carrier, and the W and

One of the large magnets being prepared for installation for the Large Hadron Collider (Courtesy of CERN)

Z bosons carry the weak nuclear force just as photons carry the electromagnetic force. The discovery of these particles had been predicted by the Standard Model and helped strengthen confidence in that theory.

In 1995, the German physicist Walter Oelert synthesized complete atoms made of antimatter by using raw material composed of the anti-quarks and anti-gluons that had been generated in a particle accelerator. In 2000, the workers at CERN created a quark-gluon plasma that is believed to resemble the condition of matter short moments after the universe began. Scientists characterize the quark-gluon plasma as a liquid though very dense—20 times denser than nuclear plasmas.

In 2002, they were able to generate large quantities of anti-hydrogen atoms—a form of antimatter. Since antimatter and normal matter are known to disintegrate when they come

Another view of one of the powerful magnets being prepared for the Large Hadron Collider (Courtesy of CERN)

into contact, the two forms of matter must be kept separate. Scientists achieved the necessary isolation by using magnetic fields to suspend a cloud of antimatter in a vacuum chamber so that the antimatter does not come into contact with normal matter.

The leaders of the CERN organization are planning to redesign the current accelerator in order to increase its power and capabilities. The enormous magnets—15 meters long and one meter wide—employed in the new machine will be wound with superconducting wires. This is the same technology that had proved unworkable during the construction of the SSC in the United States. Fortunately, scientists at CERN discovered that tiny kinks in the superconducting wire were the cause of the magnetic interference. They developed ways to check for kinks and eliminate them. Indeed, the wire wound around the huge, primary magnets is tested repeatedly for such problems.

The new version of the CERN accelerator is to be called the Large Hadron Collider (LHC). It is being installed in the same tunnel that had previously housed the Large Electron-Positron Collider (LEP) and the advanced version, LEP II. The LHC will use two acceleration tubes, one to carry protons in a clockwise rotation and the other to carry protons in a counterclockwise rotation. The tubes, placed side by side, pass through the center of the large magnets. The advanced particle detection system is located at the point where the two pathways converge and the streams of protons collide head-on. The LHC is expected to begin actual operation in 2007.

Domestic Progress

Since the 1950s, basic particle research in the United States has been dominated by the National Laboratories that are supported by the Department of Energy. Although there are 21 official facilities, only nine use their accelerators to conduct particle research. Most of the other National Laboratories use reactors for nuclear research that are similar to electrical power generators.

Brookhaven National Laboratory

Before the mid-1940s, most nuclear research was conducted in the central states such as Tennessee and the western states such as California and New Mexico. Some senior researchers resolved that the eastern states should have their own facility. Subsequently, the Brookhaven National Laboratory was founded in 1947 through the initiatives of nine prominent eastern universities. The facility is located on the edge of the village of Upton, Long Island, about 60 miles (100 km) east of New York City. Today, the laboratory is managed by a nonprofit corporation formed by Stony Brook University and the Battelle Memorial Institute of Columbus, Ohio.

An artist's concept of lead atoms colliding in an accelerator. Protons and neutrons are scattering. (Courtesy of CERN)

About 2,000 scientists and technicians are in residence at Brookhaven. Yearly, the facility hosts about 4,000 visiting scholars who stay for periods that may last up to several months. At present, the scope of research at Brookhaven is highly diversified and includes studies in the biomedical and environmental sciences.

A computer-generated image of the particle array that would come from the collision of two lead atoms (Courtesy of CERN)

The current accelerator—named the Relativistic Heavy Ion Collider (RHIC)—is the fourth generation instrument to occupy the relatively small tunnel, 2.4 mile (4.0 km) in circumference. Despite the small size of the *collider,* the researchers at Brookhaven were able to generate quark-gluon plasma before the people at CERN were able to do so. Brookhaven's successful technique employed the use of electrically charged gold atoms as the particles in the collider. When extremely heavy particles—such as gold—collide at nearly the speed of light, the collision generates an enormous burst of energy. Scientists reason that the burst of energy caused by RHIC may be comparable to the power generated by the detonation that caused the birth of the universe. The investigation of this plasma will allow physicists a better understanding of the earliest microseconds of the universe.

The research at Brookhaven has also advanced our knowledge of quarks. We now know that individual quarks are never seen in nature. Quarks are always found in triplets, or—under special circumstances—in pairs. This means that quarks are strongly attracted to one another. When broken apart, the

The new muon research facility at Brookhaven National Laboratory
(Courtesy of the Brookhaven National Laboratory)

attraction remains and the quark/gluon plasma appears to be a viscous fluid rather than a gas.

FERMI NATIONAL LABORATORY

FermiLab, as it is now known, was originally called the National Accelerator Laboratory (NAL). The Universities Research Association, a large group of universities, founded the NAL in 1967 and currently manages the facility. In 1974, the NAL was renamed to honor the great physicist Enrico Fermi. Today, FermiLab employs about 2,000 scientists and technicians.

The site of FermiLab, near town of Batavia, Illinois, occupies 6,800 acres of former farmland about 40 miles (64 km) west of Chicago. A large portion of the site has been returned to the original ecosystem by reintroducing wild grasses, wild flowers, and a small herd of buffalo.

The Tevatron, the major research instrument at FermiLab, was the world's most powerful accelerator when it became operational in 1983. The fairly small instrument is housed in a tunnel that is four miles (6.4 km) in diameter. Currently, the Tevatron is used to study the effects of colliding protons with antiprotons.

The researchers at FermiLab have tested many ideas generated by the Standard Model. The major landmarks have been the discovery of two previously undetected quarks, the so-called bottom quark in 1977 and the top quark in 1995. The negatively charged, less massive bottom quark and the positively charged, more massive top quark never appear in nature but can be produced in particle accelerators.

Although the scientists at FermiLab continue to devise new projects for their aging accelerator, they are also expanding their research into the field of astronomy. These investigations are intended to link our information concerning rare particles with our information about the origin of the universe.

ARGONNE NATIONAL LABORATORY

The site of the Argonne National Laboratory (ANL) is about 45 miles (72 km) southwest of Chicago and less than 50 miles (80 km.) from FermiLab. From its inception, the lab has been managed by the University of Chicago. Somewhat strangely, research at ANL is closer to the work of Enrico Fermi than is the research conducted at FermiLab—the facility named for him. Fermi built the first atomic reactor on the campus of the University of Chicago. The original mission of ANL was to study the chain reactions that generate reactor power. Today, ANL continues to investigate such chain reactions, while FermiLab's research no longer includes this mode of study.

At present, the scope of research at ANL is very broad, encompassing cryogenics—studying the effects of very low temperatures—the properties of exotic materials, biochemistry and other fields. Work on particle physics is a small but

Wilson Hall, the modernistic office building at Fermilab (Courtesy of the Fermi National Laboratory)

relatively important part of their mission. ANL scientists employ a small particle accelerator (less than one mile in diameter) to energize electrons. These electrons create a flood of photons that generate the most intense X-ray beams produced in the U.S. In 2006, ANL will be able to generate up to 70 beams at the same time. This innovation will allow many research projects to be undertaken at the same time.

Scientists at ANL are also planning an accelerator that will generate beams of short-lived, rare isotopes. These isotopes have either more or fewer neutrons in their nuclei than atoms of their parent element. Researchers want to know exactly what physical and chemical properties change when the number of protons and neutrons in the nucleus of an atom are modified. Physicists hope that this facility will help overcome the research problems caused by the short life span of some isotopes. They plan to hold such short-lived isotopes in a super-cooled chamber called a gas catcher cell as a way to prolong their life spans.

LAWRENCE BERKELEY NATIONAL LABORATORY

The Lawrence Berkeley National Laboratory (LBNL) is adjacent to the campus of the University of California at Berkeley. The arrival of Ernest O. Lawrence in the 1930s helped promote particle physics research at the university. Shortly after his arrival, he built the first small cyclotron and studies in particle physics soon became ever more popular. However, the federal government did not support the University of California with major subsidies until the 1950s. At that time, research opportunities were expanded and the Bevatron was designed. When it was completed in 1954, the Bevatron was the largest accelerator in the world.

Leon Lederman is the director emeritus of Fermilab, where he was working when he won the Nobel Prize in physics for his studies of neutrinos. (Courtesy of the Fermi National Laboratory)

More than 50 years later, the Bevatron is obsolete and scientists and administrators at the University of California are recycling the facility. The original round building, about 300 feet (100 m) in diameter, is now used to house a more modern accelerator in which electrons reach near–light speed by the use of huge modern magnets. At certain points in the circular track, the electrons interact with pulses of radio waves. This contact causes the electrons to emit a huge number of photons. An X-ray beam is composed of a cluster of photons and a high concentration of these particles produces a very intense beam. Beams formed in this manner are so-called "soft" X-rays because of their relatively low frequency. They can be focused in much the same way that light beams are focused by a lens. When an intense beam is narrowed by focusing, it is ideal for imaging the interior parts of bodily cells and for detecting the presence of tiny traces of chemicals. Most of the research

The Isotope Catcher at the Argonne National Laboratory is supercooled by liquid helium to slow the loss of radioactivity in short-lived isotopes. (Courtesy of the Argonne National Laboratory)

now being done at LBNL has such practical applications. Consequently, taxpayers are obtaining a return on their original investment in the Lawrence Berkeley National Laboratory.

STANFORD

The current picture of high energy physics research at Stanford University is more than a bit complicated. Initially, the center piece of this National Laboratory was the two mile long (3.2 km) Stanford Linear Accelerator Center (SLAC) which had been built in the 1960s. The accelerator was able to drive electrons at near–light speed into targets composed of hydrogen and deuterium atoms. The spray of particles that resulted from the collisions gave the first solid clues about the existence of quarks in 1968.

In 1972, the university built the Stanford Positron Electron Circular Accelerator Ring (SPEAR), which also used a beam of electrons as the main energy carrier. The new accelerator also revealed new information about the nature of quarks.

A modification of the SPEAR ring began in the late 1970s. This change allowed that facility to generate electrons. Eventually, the modified linear accelerator would be used to generate beams of both electrons and positrons. By the early 1990s, the upgraded ring system would allow the two distinct beams to flow in opposite directions. The two beams can now be made to collide in the center of BaBar—the new, high-capacity detector system.

An inside view of the tunnel housing the linear accelerator (Courtesy of the Stanford Linear Accelerator Center)

In 2001, the SLAC researchers observed a small difference between the disintegration rates of electrons and positrons. The positrons, which are antiparticles, disintegrate at a slightly faster rate than the electrons. Although scientists believe that the two types of particles were produced in equal numbers when the universe was young, the antiparticles are no longer present in the natural universe. Astrophysicists reason that the small difference in the rate of disintegration may account for the absence of antiparticles. Since the faster disintegrating antiparticles (the positrons) were never generated (except in particle accelerators) after the *big bang,* the slower disintegrating particles (the electrons) quickly filled the universe.

At present, the research at SLAC is focused on the ultimate fate of the so-called B mesons. Mesons, composed of quarks and anti-quarks, are very interactive force carriers and are believed to influence the interactions among protons and neutrons in the atomic nucleus.

THE THOMAS JEFFERSON NATIONAL ACCELERATOR FACILITY

Known now as the JLab, the Thomas Jefferson Accelerator Facility is located in suburban Newport News, Virginia, near the mouth of the James River. The facility is the most recent addition to the group of National Laboratories currently dedicated to the study of high energy physics. Regional pride and politics probably played a part in the founding of this facility—as they had in the development of the 1947 founding of the Brookhaven National Laboratory. That effort was launched by administrators and scientists from a collection of universities in the southeastern United States. The group now contains over 60 such institutions from the District of Columbia and 17 states (including, somewhat oddly, Massachusetts). The facility management team is called Southern Universities Research Association (SURA) and has its offices in D.C.

An aerial view of the site of the Thomas Jefferson National Laboratory
(Courtesy of the Thomas Jefferson National Laboratory)

After several years of planning and proposal preparation, the JLab was funded by the Department of Energy in the early 1980s. The construction of living quarters for the staff and a building to house the Concentrated Electron Beam Accelerator Facility (CEBAF) was soon begun. The building of the facility required about 10 years and the first experiments were conducted in 1994. The original CEBAF had two linear tunnels about 1,200 feet (400 m) in length and 480 feet (160 m) apart. To begin a project, electrons were injected into the left chamber and then accelerated by the superconducting magnets. The electrons coasted through a semicircular connecting tube and then entered the right linear accelerator chamber. Here, they were again accelerated. At the end of the tunnel, the electron stream could be aimed at one of three targets by way of three diversion channels. Each such channel had its own *detector* system. This system recorded the path and energy of the sub-atomic particles that had been generated when the electron beam struck the selected target.

Almost as soon as the accelerator was running properly, plans were laid to augment its capabilities. The first modification was the installation of a fourth diversion channel into which the electron beam could be directed. This option allowed the beam to power a laser that emitted concentrated ultraviolet light. By focusing the concentrated light, the laser could be used to etch solid materials. For example, such lasers can etch very accurate microcircuits on ceramic chips.

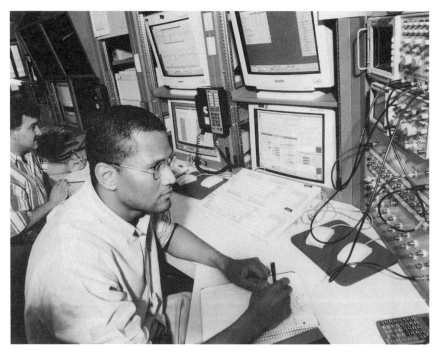

The control room for the accelerator at the Thomas Jefferson National Laboratory (Courtesy of the Thomas Jefferson National Laboratory)

Soon, an infrared laser was installed. Both types of lasers have practical industrial applications. Thus, the laboratory directors helped ensure continuing support from the government by generating both basic knowledge and practical technologies.

Next, a second semicircular connecting tube was constructed at the base of the right linear channel. The tube captured the unused electrons and sent them back into the electron flow. This recycling demonstrated the practicality of the laboratory managers. All parties were pleased when this idea proved to save both electricity and money.

Experiments using the electron accelerator have also added information about the nature of quarks. The possible sighting of a particle composed of five quarks was an exciting event for the scientists at JLab. According to the Standard Model, such a particle is mathematically possible but, previously, all sightings had been ambiguous.

Finally, in 2003, Department of Energy officials decided to double the power of the electron beam by adding new, stronger magnets to the linear segments and constructing another detector assembly. Scientists hope that the forthcoming increase in the accelerator's power will either reveal the full nature of such a five-quark particle or prove that no such particle exists.

CORNELL UNIVERSITY

The Cornell Electron Storage Ring (CESR) and its associated research tools are not a part of the National Laboratory system. Cornell's high energy physics research is an example of the independent investigations conducted on university campuses across the nation. Cornell's work is distinguished by its early entrance into this field, its high level of research productivity, and its continuity of participation despite limited economic resources.

Called the Hall, this is where the beam channels are directed to their targets. (Courtesy of the Thomas Jefferson National Laboratory)

In the 1930s, Cornell recruited Stanley Livingston from Ernest Lawrence's group at the University of California at Berkeley. Livingston came to Ithaca, New York, knowing how to build a cyclotron—and immediately set about doing so. Livingston's device was small, as were all other cyclotrons at that time. Over the years, the instrument grew into a double-channel storage ring about half a mile (1 km) in diameter. One ring stores electrons that move in a counterclockwise stream. The other ring stores positrons that move in a clockwise motion. After several circuits—to build up their velocity—the beams are collided in the center of a large detector. The electron beam is also used to generate both X-rays and intense ultraviolet light beams. The two types of radiation can be used to explore the inner structure of molecules such as complex proteins.

One of the most recent accomplishments at Cornell was the use of the very brief, very bright X-ray flashes to make images of a chemical reaction in progress. By scattering the X-rays off the surface of the water in a laboratory vessel, scientists were able to see the pattern of movement of the electrons in the chemical reaction. Each frame in their "movie" was just four quintillionths of a second in duration. Another accomplishment was imaging the RNA strands that allow some infectious viruses to reproduce. Knowledge of viruses' RNA can lead to specific antiviral treatments.

The Injector is the source of the electrons that are energized in the accelerator. (Courtesy of the Thomas Jefferson National Laboratory)

An Overall Perspective

Hans Bethe, the joke-loving Nobel Prize winner, helped maintain the strong research capabilities at the Floyd R. Newman Laboratory for Elementary Particle Physics at Cornell University. (Courtesy of the U.S. National Archives and Record Administration)

Many physicists were discouraged when Congress canceled the construction of the Superconducting Super Collider. Some thought that public interest in particle physics had weakened when the threat of nuclear war declined. Scientists worried that physics may seem relevant only if it is a crucial element in national security. When that danger was reduced, many people questioned the practical results of physics research. Nevertheless, the government has continued to fund the National Laboratories (although at a lower rate). Physicists are pleased that these institutions are able to sustain their involvement in the research of high energy physics. Nevertheless, the recent accomplishments of European physicists may worry some of the ambitious scientists in the United States.

A second concern might be the fact that scientists at the National Laboratories must change their priorities and spend less time on pure, basic science and more time on potentially commercial technologies. However, in the history of science, work toward practical goals can often advance basic knowledge.

12
The Cosmic Connection

Since the turn of the 21st century, some important areas of basic scientific research and theory development have been brought into progressively closer contact. For example, biologists are integrating studies in such fields as molecular genetics, cell biology, and embryology. Physical scientists are undertaking a similar process in the fields of nuclear physics and astronomy. One of the topics that links physics and astronomy is the study of cosmic rays. These rays are a source of high energy particles that come from outer space.

At present, high energy particles can be produced artificially. But before E. O. Lawrence invented the cyclotron in 1930, studies of high energy particles were limited to the investigation of cosmic rays. The natural energy level of cosmic rays approximates and sometimes even exceeds the energy level reached by particles in some modern accelerators. However, cosmic ray particles are scattered rather than focused. Therefore, the number of particle collisions recorded by cosmic ray detectors—such as cloud chambers—is lower and the effects of the collisions are difficult to interpret. Consequently, advanced study of subatomic particles is now done almost exclusively using powerful accelerators. Nevertheless, the study of cosmic rays resulted in some major scientific advances in the 1930s.

For example, in 1930, Carl Anderson—then a young instructor at the California Institute of Technology (Cal Tech)—

discovered the positron (an anti-electron) in a stream of cosmic rays. He had constructed his own cloud chamber to record the tracks of the energetic particles coming from outer space. Anderson had seen many protons come into the chamber and knew the length of their tracks. One day, he saw the track of a positively charged particle that was ten times longer than a typical proton track. Anderson reasoned that this long track must have been made by a previously undetected particle. Further study showed that the new particle had the same characteristics as a particle proposed by the English physicist Paul Dirac in 1926. Dirac had predicted the existence of such an object based on theory and had called it a positron. To honor him, Anderson retained that name for his own discovery.

In 1937, while using the cloud chamber at Cal Tech, J. C. Street and I. C. Stevenson discovered the *muon*—a type of heavy electron. Although the discoveries of the positron and the muon were impressive, more laboratory investigations and astronomical observations were needed before the importance of these findings could be completely understood.

We now know that cosmic rays are harmless, energized, subatomic particles. Most of the particles are protons, the nuclei that remain after atoms of hydrogen are stripped of their single electrons. Most of the remaining subatomic particles found in cosmic rays are known as Alpha particles, the nuclei of helium atoms (composed of two protons and two neutrons). Some cosmic ray particles are free electrons and some are the nuclei of all the other elements. The heavier elements are relatively rare among cosmic particles but, interestingly, are present in about the same proportion as they are in the Sun's atmosphere.

Scientists believe that the atomic nuclei found in cosmic rays are energized by powerful magnetic fields. These magnetic fields are formed when a star dies. The death of a huge star—one larger than the Sun—causes a tremendously bright flash of light that is called a supernova and usually involves a violent expansion and subsequent contraction of the substance that formed the star. This expansion and contraction leaves a very energetic cloud of material that moves away from the collapsing core of the dying star. The cloud contains subatomic particles from the body of the star and remnants of the star's strong magnetic field. This magnetic field raises the velocity of the particles to nearly the speed of light. The particles escape the gravitational pull of the remnants of the star and speed away in all directions. The cloud and its magnetic fields dim slowly over time but can continue to exist for thousands of years.

In addition to nuclear particles, the rays also include some very energetic photons (the carriers of light energy) in the frequency range of gamma rays. Night and day, the amount of gamma ray activity in the sky is highly uniform. Detectors, such as those using photographic film, reveal that these rays exist in broad showers of invisible light that emanates from every part of the sky. However, about once a day, there is an exception to the general uniformity. During these periods, very strong gamma rays flash for about two seconds or less. These flashes are known as gamma hot spots or gamma bursts and, as yet, are difficult for astrophysicists to explain.

The gamma bursts were discovered by accident. In the 1960s, government scientists sought to detect the effects of the radiation caused by any secretive tests of atomic weapons. The United States government placed gamma ray detectors aboard the Vela family of spy satellites to monitor for nuclear detonations prohibited by international test ban agreements of 1963. In 1967, one of the gamma ray detectors registered a strong signal that clearly was not from a nuclear weapon detonation. This phenomenon had no connection with national security but news of the observation was classified as top secret. Although national security analysts were mystified by the characteristics of the signal, the scientific community was not informed of the problem until 1973.

Meanwhile, in 1971, the National Aeronautics and Space Administration (NASA) launched a satellite to monitor sun spots and sun flares. While not programmed to do so, the computer also recorded several gamma bursts. A similar satellite was launched later in the same year and a computer again recorded strong, short-duration gamma ray bursts. Government officials finally turned to physicists to locate the origin of these phenomena. The scientists confirmed that the bursts came from outer space. Ironically, the following year, the findings were further confirmed by studies published by Soviet scientists. Thereafter, scientists established an international register of gamma ray burst events and an accounting procedure to document such events. At present, worldwide detectors pick up an average of one burst a day—year after year.

Today, American and Russian scientists believe that gamma bursts and other types of cosmic rays are caused by explosions that occur at the moment a star dies. They argue that an unusually intense burst signifies the death of an exceedingly large star. A black hole—a very dense, little-understood stellar object—may be another result of such a violent explosion. Study of the detailed patterns of such bursts and the X-ray flares that arise after the formation of a black hole could reveal much information about the origin and the fate of the cosmos.

Expansion and Contraction

In a series of studies in the late 1920s and early 1930s, Edwin Hubble documented the fact that the universe is expanding. He also proposed that the galaxies farthest from the Earth are moving outward at an increasing rate of speed. To reach this conclusion, Hubble used a fact that had been known for years—that light energy emitted by the stars was redder than was expected. The color red has the longest wavelength in the color spectrum and Hubble concluded that this meant the stars were moving away from the Earth. As the stars moved farther away, their wavelengths were stretched and the color of their emanations became a redder hue.

Hubble's studies also revealed that the universe was much larger than had been previously accepted. Before Hubble's proof, astronomers believed that the Milky Way, our own galaxy, constituted the entire universe. Hubble showed that the so-called nebula, thought to be wispy formations that were part of the Milky Way, were actually galaxies in their own right. These galaxies contained millions of stars and existed millions of light years from the Milky Way.

The acceptance of a much larger, far more dynamic universe was a positive step toward solving the problem of how and when the universe began. The second important step was made in 1964 by two young physicists working at Bell Laboratories in Passaic, New Jersey. Arno Penzias and Robert Woodrow Wilson accidentally discovered cosmic background radiation signals in the frequency range of microwaves—electromagnetic waves with a fairly long wavelength. The two young men made their discovery while testing an antenna that was programmed to receive signals from communication satellites. They repeatedly heard a faint but steady signal that could not be identified. After eliminating all other possible sources, they concluded that the signal echoed the reverberations caused eons ago by the birth of the universe.

Their conclusion tied in with another speculation about the events at the earliest stages of the universe. This idea was supported by George Gamow, a Ukrainian physicist born in 1904. By the early 1930s, he was a physics professor at Leningrad University. In 1934, Gamow was allowed to leave the Soviet Union to attend a scientific meeting in Belgium. He secretly left the meeting and escaped to the United States, where he remained for the rest of his life. Gamow soon became a professor of physics at George Washington University in Washington, D.C.

In 1948, Gamow wrote a paper that advanced the idea that the universe began as a single, sudden event. His theory was not well accepted by cosmologists and the disrespectful term "big bang" was coined by those who opposed the idea. Over the ensuing years, however, the name lost its negative connotations and became the term used to describe the most widely accepted theory about the origin of the universe.

If the universe had begun from the force of an ordinary explosion, it would not be surprising that the stars—made from material at the site of the explosion—would be widely dispersed and continue to move apart. However, as time passed and the debris moved farther from the center of the blast, the material should have moved more slowly and finally come to rest. Yet the big bang was not an ordinary happening. Theorists believe that a minuscule, exceedingly dense, infinitely hot speck—smaller than a pinhead—was the object responsible for the creation and release of an enormous amount of energy. The waves of energy expanded outward in a process called inflation. Today, when the velocity of the outward-moving celestial bodies is measured, it shows that the rate of expansion seems to be increasing. Indeed, the celestial objects most distant from the Earth are receding more rapidly than the nearer objects.

In 1917, a number of years before Hubble's discovery, Albert Einstein encountered a major frustration while working on his general theory of relativity. Although all his calculations seemed logical, his equations led to the conclusion that the force of gravity was pulling all the objects in the universe toward one another and that the universe was slowly contracting. Einstein was greatly distressed with this result because he was convinced that the universe was static. Therefore, Einstein added a mathematical factor that he called Lambda (a letter in the Greek alphabet). Just as he had hoped, the addition of the Lambda constant allowed a computational result that seemingly counteracted the force of gravity and thereby confirmed his idea of a static universe. Nevertheless, Einstein was not completely satisfied with his solution. He was aware that he would be criticized for introducing an "artificial" factor that would help verify his theory.

Years later, Einstein learned of Hubble's idea that the universe was expanding. After careful study, he accepted Hubble's theory and concluded that his own hypothesis of a static universe was incorrect. Today, scientists use the expression "dark energy" to help explain why the universe, contrary to force of natural gravity, has continued to expand. They are cautious, however, about applying that term, because of its frequent and misleading use in science fiction books and movies.

Caution is also prevalent when scientists discuss how the force of gravity affects the galaxies relatively close to the Earth. In this context, the force of gravity seems more powerful than would be expected. When a cluster of five or six massive galaxies is studied, it is apparent that the pull of natural gravity is, indeed, drawing them together. Precise measurements show that the galaxies are coming together at a faster rate than their detectable mass would have predicted.

The key to this mystery may be the term *detectable mass*. The best explanation for the unexpected velocity seems to be that each galaxy has far more mass than previously recognized. Since the source of this additional mass cannot be seen astrophysicists use the term dark matter.

Scientists admit that the use of the similar terms *dark energy* and *dark matter* can be somewhat confusing. Dark energy refers to a force that counters gravity and repels objects away from one another, while dark matter works with gravity and draws objects together. Theorists try to explain this contradiction by saying that dark energy affects the entire universe while dark matter exerts an influence on celestial bodies that are closer to the Earth. In any case, these terms remain ambiguous.

Dark matter is more likely to be cleared up soon. Many reasonable ideas have been advanced to account for the missing mass. For example, new studies show that neutrinos probably do have a small amount of mass. Since the universe seems full of invisible neutrinos, it is plausible that they account for a large share of such mass.

Some of the invisible bodies might be much larger than a neutrino. For example, black holes are supermassive objects but they are only detectable by their effects on other bodies or the materials in range of their gravitational pull. They cannot be seen directly by any telescope. Consequently, many black holes could exist but their enormous masses would not be included in the astrophysicists' computations.

Other sun- and planet-sized bodies can exist that give off no visible light. A star that has not achieved ignition would be one such object. Such dim stars are called brown dwarfs.

In the early 1990s, scientists at the Jet Propulsion Laboratory (JPL) in California began to look for dark matter by scanning the sky for objects radiating in the infrared range of light frequencies. Such objects are normally invisible through an ordinary telescope. The JPL scientists found tantalizing clues but

Chandra *is the satellite X-ray observatory launched by NASA to locate strong X-ray emanations from outer space.* (Courtesy of the National Aeronautics and Space Administration)

could record few positive sightings with the equipment then available. However, the astrophysicists at the National Aeronautics and Space Administration (NASA) determined that the orbiting, multi-functional *Hubble Space Telescope* might furnish new clues about the nature of such matter. The scientists programmed the *Hubble* to search for examples of the so-called halo phenomena. When a dark object—such as a brown dwarf—is in a line between the bright object and a telescope, the farther object is obscured except for a circle of light—the halo—radiating around the body of the dim star. Such halos were not easily visible.

Previously, this phenomenon had been observed only fleetingly, during routine astronomical surveys. In 2001, a few halos were, indeed, sighted by the *Hubble Space Telescope.* These first authenticated sightings of the halo phenomena caused researchers to plan the launch of a different satellite that would carry a newly developed, highly specialized infrared telescope. Their goal was achieved in 2003 when the *Spitzer Space Telescope* was sent into orbit. The new telescope quickly confirmed that the halo phenomenon is caused by presence of a brown dwarf or other very dim celestial body. Today, the Spitzer is scanning the sky for other dim objects and has located more than had been previously expected. Astrophysicists now believe that at least some portion of the so-called missing mass is composed of many millions of very dim, sun- or planet-sized objects that are invisible to ordinary detectors. The scientists acknowledge that there remains an incomplete understanding of the material that makes up the missing mass.

A much different approach is directed toward a detailed understanding of gravitational waves. Einstein's general relativity theory and the Standard Model assume that the force of gravity is carried by particles (called gravitons) that are similar to the photons that carry light energy. Photons travel in waves and scientists believe that gravitons may also travel in waves. However, neither gravitons nor gravitational waves have been

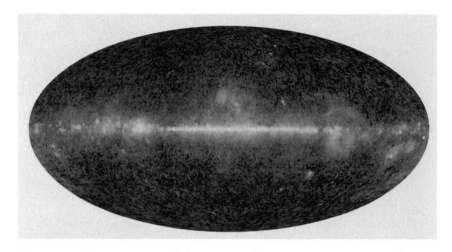

This is a preliminary map of the very small variations in energy in the cosmic background microwave radiation. (Courtesy of the National Aeronautics and Space Administration)

actually observed. Researchers at NASA and other worldwide organizations are working to develop a means to detect these particles. The problem is that gravity is a very weak force and its effects are masked by other, more powerful forces such as that of electromagnetism. Also, gravitational waves are presumed to have very long wavelengths so that their detectors must be able to monitor a huge area.

NASA's prospective solution to this problem involves the launch of three spacecraft. Their flight away from the Earth's magnetic field will be programmed to position the ships into the configuration of an equilateral triangle with sides that measure millions of miles in length. A robotic spacecraft will be stationed at each vertex of the imaginary triangle—the point at which two sides of a triangle intersect—and laser beams from each craft will be focused on the other two spaceships. If a gravitational wave should pass between any two of the space vehicles, the laser beam connecting them will be disturbed and the gravitational wave will leave a record of its passing. An understanding of gravitational waves would be gained from these records that would permit a more comprehensive picture of the early universe.

In another effort to understand the dynamics of the universe as a whole, NASA instituted the Wilkinson Microwave Anisotropy Probe (WMAP) in 2000. This program is aimed at measuring and understanding the tiny fluctuations in temperature that may have been present when the universe was young. The probe is carried out by sampling the background microwave radiation in each tiny section of the sky. The background microwave radiation is the remnant of the big bang discovered by the Bell Laboratory scientists in 1964. The antenna tuned to the microwave frequency can detect any temperature variations from section to section. A chart showing the very small variations in temperature across the entire sky is called an anisotropy map. The map will provide astrophysicists with clues about the state of the universe before the existence of tangible matter.

Other Collaborations

Most research on high energy particles takes place in the National Laboratories that are funded by the U.S. Department of Energy. Three ongoing projects that involve scientists and administrators from the FermiLab near Chicago, Illinois, demonstrate the overlapping interests of particle physicists and astronomers. One is the Sloan Digital Sky Survey, an ambitious project that will catalog the many millions stars in one quarter of the sky. A group of institutions, both National Laboratories and universities, is involved in the project that is funded, in part, by the Alfred E. Sloan Foundation. The home base of the project is at the Apache Point Observatory in New Mexico, in the Sacramento Mountains near Alamogordo where the first nuclear weapon was tested.

The project is using a telescope that was designed and built mainly by scientists and engineers from Princeton University. The telescope was transported and reassembled at the observatory operated by the University of New Mexico. The goal of the survey is a detailed census of all the celestial objects in the survey area. Location and apparent brightness of comets, asteroids, stars, and entire galaxies will be recorded. Neighborhood setting will also be noted. For example, some galaxies such as the ones shaped like flat spirals seem to be in areas in space that are relatively thinly populated. The scientists will look for stars that have spectrums that indicate that they have relatively low quantities of the metallic elements. Such stars are believed to be very old—among the first stars that formed when the universe was young. In sum, the researchers expect many new insights into all the stages in the history of the universe.

The telescope for the Sloan Observatory is specially designed to be able to cover a wide field of view with precision. (Courtesy of the Fermi National Laboratory)

The second project is focused on obtaining a more direct measurement of dark energy. A special infrared camera will be aligned with the four-meter telescope at the Cerro Tololo Observatory in northern Chile. The broad goal is to gain a more precise measure of the expansion rate of the universe. Thirty thousand of the most distant galaxies will be observed and their light spectrums will be analyzed to determine their rate of outward movement. Again, the participants involved in this

The cosmic ray detectors are being readied for installation in the broad area set aside for the Pierre Auger Observatory. (Courtesy of the Fermi National Laboratory)

endeavor will include physicists and astronomers from several National Laboratories and universities. Team members expect to begin observations with the new camera in 2008.

The third undertaking is a cosmic ray observatory being constructed in Argentina that will cover an area of 1,200 square miles (3,072 square km). The project is called the Pierre Auger Collaboration, in honor of the French physicist who pioneered cosmic ray research in the 1920s and 1930s. The focus of the project is the analysis of the rare cosmic ray particles that carry very high energy. These particles are thousands of times less frequent and thousands of times more energetic than the ordinary protons that make up most of the cosmic ray particles, and their origins are totally unknown.

Such extremely energetic particles never reach the surface of the Earth. Upon entering the upper atmosphere, they inevitably strike an atmospheric particle and both particles disintegrate. So much energy is imparted by the collision that the fragments go on to collide with other particles lower in the atmosphere. The overall result is a shower of thousands of particle fragments.

When completed, the observatory will have two types of detectors. One type is an ultraviolet light monitor with a wide field of view. Four of these monitors are being placed at the corners of the observatory area. When the high energy fragments interact with normal atmospheric nitrogen, the nitrogen atoms fluoresce in the ultraviolet frequencies. When an ultraviolet flare appears, these detectors register that event and signal the main computer.

The second type of detector registers the arrival of the particles in the particle shower when they reach the Earth's surface. The scientists will emplace 1,600 of these special detectors one mile (about 1.5 km) apart in regular rows to cover the 1,200 square miles (3,072 sq km) of the observatory space. Each of these special particle detectors is a rigid plastic tank four feet (1.5 m) high and 12 feet (4 m) in diameter. Each holds 300 gallons (1,135 l) of purified water. Inside are three sensitive light detectors. When particles from the high energy shower arrive, they will generate a flash of light when they enter the water. The flash will be detected and reported via a radio transmitter to the central computer.

The detectors are mainly self-sufficient. A solar panel provides electricity that is stored in a compact battery. The status of each detector will be monitored electronically so that routine maintenance of the large array of the devises can be minimized.

The detectors began to register hits in 2005. In fact, the research staff, which numbers approximately 250, mainly part-time, scientists from 14 countries, is receiving more information than they expected.

Now that new information is beginning to come in, the scientists judge that the origin of the very high energy particles must be relatively close to our galaxy because particles lose energy as they pass through space. If the particles came from extreme distances, it would be hard to believe that they could retain so much energy by the time they reach Earth. While new clues are coming in rapidly and new theories are being generated, the researchers still decline to speculate about the true origins of these particles. When the answers are finally available, everyone will know more about the nature of the universe.

Glossary

acceleration   An increase in velocity. At the level of nuclear particles, it also means an increase in the energy of the particle.

alpha particle   A single particle formed by two protons and two neutrons joined together; identical to the atomic nucleus of helium, the particle has a positive electrical charge.

antimatter   Matter that is a mirror image of ordinary matter, with opposite properties such as electric charge.

atom   The unit of a chemical element that consists of a massive central nucleus around which electrons move in variable orbits.

beta particle   An electron, specifically one emitted at high speed by an atom undergoing radioactive disintegration.

big bang   The cataclysmic event believed to have been the origin of the universe about 14 billion years ago.

Bohr model   An equation that predicts that an atom will emit electromagnetic radiation when an electron circling the nucleus jumps from one energy level to another—the so-called quantum jump. The idea was crucial for the advance of theoretical atomic physics.

B quarks   The bottom quark. One of the fundamental constituents of matter.

breeder reactor   A nuclear reactor that produces more fissionable material than it consumes; used to produce useful quantities of plutonium from uranium.

bubble chamber   A detector of nuclear particles; when moving through certain liquids the particles trigger the formation of bubbles that correspond to the track of the particle.

chain reaction   The process that takes place when neutrons released by radioactive materials strike the nuclei of adjacent atoms and produce two or more new neutrons.

collider   A particle accelerator that allows two beams of particles to collide head-on.

control rod   A long metal cylinder several inches in diameter that can be inserted into the core of a nuclear reactor to absorb excess neutrons and control the rate of atomic disintegration.

cosmic radiation   Very penetrating radiation that reaches Earth from outer space; it consists mainly of protons.

curie   The unit of radioactivity equal to the activity of one gram of radium; about one trillion particles per second.

cyclotron   A machine that accelerates heavy particles such as atomic nuclei along a circular track to speeds at which the nuclei or target atoms disintegrate on impact. The disintegration products reveal the inner structure of atoms.

decay   The breakdown of an atomic nucleus that releases protons and neutrons and energy.

detector   Any device that can detect the presence of a particle or nuclear fragment and measure one or more of its physical properties.

deuterium   A hydrogen atom with one proton and one neutron in its nucleus—often called heavy hydrogen.

down   A quark that has one-third the negative charge of an electron.

electromagnetic force   A long-range force associated with electric and magnetic properties of particles. It is mediated by photons.

electron   The small, indivisible particle that carries a negative charge of electricity.

electron volt   A measure of kinetic energy; a way of describing the effective mass of a charged particle under acceleration.

element   A substance that consists of only one type of atom.

fission   The splitting of the nucleus of an atom, usually by the action of neutron bombardment, into two roughly equal parts accompanied by a release of energy and the production of additional neutrons.

gamma radiation   A product of radioactivity that consists of radiation similar to X-rays.

gaseous diffusion   A technique for separating atoms that are chemically identical but vary slightly in weight by the use of a porous membrane or filtering device.

Geiger counter   A device for measuring the amount of radiation in a particular location by detecting the electrical effects of the radiation.

GeV   Giga electron volts. One billion volts. Scientists use this term because billion is not a standard word in many languages.

gluon   The particle that carries the color force that binds quarks.

Grand Unified Theory (GUT)   A mathematical theory by which all natural forces are seen as aspects of a single force. The formulation of this theory is incomplete.

hadron   Particles such as protons and neutrons then are composed of quarks.

half-life   The time required for a given mass of radioactive material to disintegrate to half the original amount.

heavy water   Water in which the normal hydrogen atoms have been replaced by deuterium atoms, making the chemical formulation D_2O rather than H_2O.

high-level waste   This class of nuclear waste is defined by its source: High-level waste comes from spent fuel rods and from weapon disassembly.

infrared   Invisible light having a wavelength longer than visible light and associated with a source of heat.

ion   An atom that is not in electrical balance; one that has too many or too few electrons to balance the positive charge of the nucleus.

isotope   An atom that has a nucleus with surplus neutrons.

lepton An elementary particle that responds to the weak force but not the strong force. The six known leptons are the electron, muon, tau, and their three associated neutrinos.

linear accelerator A particle accelerator in which the particles travel in a straight path.

low-level waste This class of nuclear waste is defined by what it is not: It is all waste that is not high-level waste. A more useful definition used in some states is waste that will cease to generate radiation in fewer than 500 years.

luminosity A measure of the frequency of collisions in a particle accelerator.

moderator The material used in a nuclear reactor to slow down neutrons and thus make them more likely to strike the nucleus of a nearby atom.

molecule The smallest bit of matter that is composed of two or more atoms.

muon A particle that appears to be identical with an electron except for its greater mass.

neutrino Any of three uncharged and virtually massless particles.

neutron A particle having slightly more mass than a proton but no electrical charge.

nuclear reactor A structure that permits the chain reaction of nuclear fission to be maintained and controlled.

nucleus The tiny, dense core of an atom composed of neutrons and protons held together by the strong force.

photon A massless unit of electromagnetic radiation, such as visible light.

positron A particle having the same mass as an electron but with the opposite electrical charge.

plutonium A synthetic radioactive metal element; it is made available in useful quantities only by the irradiation of uranium in a nuclear furnace (breeder reactor).

proton A massive particle that carries a positive electrical charge; the particle that forms the nucleus of hydrogen.

quarks Any of six fractionally charged elementary particles the respond to the strong force and that appear to exist only in combinations of two or three.

radioactivity The property possessed by some elements for spontaneous atomic disintegration that produces alpha and beta particles and gamma radiation.

scintillation counter A device used to measure the strength of radioactivity by counting the flashes or sparks produced on a phosphorescent surface.

Standard Model The current theory of the interactions of elementary particles.

strong force The force that holds the atomic nucleus together.

superconductivity The ability of some materials to maintain perpetual electric currents without heat or energy loss because the materials have no resistance to the flow of electric current.

synchrotron A type of cyclotron; a machine for accelerating electrons or positrons in a circular path by means of electromagnetic pulses.

uranium The metallic element that has 92 protons but an excess of 41 or more neutrons. Uranium with 43 extra neutrons is capable of undergoing spontaneous fission.

uranium hexafluoride A molecule having one atom of uranium and six atoms of fluorine that exists as a gas at room temperature. This gas is used to separate the isotopes of uranium by the gaseous diffusion method.

X-rays A penetrating electromagnetic radiation that can be generated by colliding high energy electrons with a metal wafer (usually tungsten). The energetic collision generates a flow of photons that carry the electromagnetic force.

Further Reading

Allison, Graham. *Nuclear Terrorism: The Ultimate Preventable Catastrophe.* New York: Times Books, 2004. An outstanding political scientist's views of the threat and the policies and procedures intended to suppress it.

Asimov, Isaac. *Atom.* New York: Dutton, 1991. Asimov was one of the most productive authors ever to write science fiction and popular works of science. *Atom* is one of his major achievements, covering current atomic science from the composition of all matter to speculations on the beginning and ending of the universe—all in a highly readable form.

Berger, Melvin. *Atoms, Molecules and Quarks.* New York: G. P. Putnam's Sons, 1986. This book is a good brief presentation of the major scientific facts of atomic studies. It follows a historical sequence that takes the reader to the search for quarks and other exotic particles. Well illustrated with black-and-white drawings, it includes a good sample of simple, safe experiments that illuminate some basic phenomena using kitchen equipment.

Bergeron, Kenneth D. *Tritium on Ice: The Dangerous New Alliance of Nuclear Weapons and Nuclear Power.* Cambridge, Mass.: The MIT Press, 2004. The use of uranium fuel for nuclear power plants as a source of tritium, the trigger material for the H bomb, is denounced as highly risky.

Burgan, Michael, Nancy Cohen, et al. *Nuclear Energy* (Discovery Channel School Science). Milwaukee, Wis.: Gareth Stevens Publishing, 2002. This book provides a good background for young readers on the beginnings of the nuclear age and the development of nuclear energy, including the problem of radioactive waste.

Cobb, Vicki. *Why Doesn't the Sun Burn Out?* New York: Lodestar, 1990. This is a relatively relaxed and informal approach to some aspects of basic physics. For example, the illustrations are in the form of cartoons. Important concepts are presented in an easily understood manner. Included are several hands-on experiments that readers can conduct themselves.

Cooper, Christopher. *Matter.* New York: DK Publishing, 1992. This history of atomic science and other areas of physics is presented in a straightforward manner and illustrated by color photographs. Geared to a young adult reading level.

Daley, Michael. *Nuclear Power: Promise or Peril.* Minneapolis, Minn.: Lerner Publications Company, 1997. This book deals directly with public policies related to the generation of electricity by the use of atomic fission. It provides arguments from both the pronuclear and antinuclear perspectives by scientists and ordinary citizens.

Heaberlin, Scott W. *A Case for Nuclear-Generated Electricity.* Columbus, Ohio: Battelle Press, 2003. Using an easy, conversational style, the author lays out the specifics of nuclear science and power generation.

Henderson, Harry. *Nuclear Physics.* New York: Facts On File, Inc. 1998. A clear, down-to-earth presentation of the research work that led to the nuclear age.

Leventhal, Paul, ed. *Nuclear Power and the Spread of Nuclear Weapons: Can We Have One Without the Other.* Washington, D.C.: Potomac Books, 2002. This book is a compilation of articles and essays by established experts that covers a wide range of related topics, from shortages of electricity to nuclear proliferation.

Maruki, Toshi. *Hiroshima No Pika.* New York: William Morrow & Co., 1982. A firsthand account of the devastation—physical, biological, and psychological—from an atomic bomb attack. It yields a strong argument in favor of nuclear disarmament.

Medvedev, Zhores A. *The Legacy of Chernobyl.* New York: W. W. Norton & Co., 1992. A classic analysis of the causes and consequences of the Chernobyl tragedy.

Morris, Robert C. *The Environmental Case for Nuclear Power: Economic, Medical, and Political Considerations.* New York: Continuum International Publishing Group, 2000. The author, a retired chemistry teacher, argues that energy from fossil fuels is polluting and that renewable means are not feasible or too costly. He says this means that we must make room for some nuclear facilities in a full set of electric power providers.

Penrose, Roger. *The Road to Reality: A Complete Guide to the Laws of the Universe*. New York: Knopf, 2005. Containing a solid dose of mathematics, this is not an easy book, but it can be digested in small bites and provides substantial rewards for those who work through it.

Veltman, Martinus J. G. *Facts and Mysteries in Elementary Particle Physics*. Singapore: World Scientific Publishing Company, 2003. Oriented for lay readers by a true expert (author is the 1999 Nobel Prize winner in physics), this book covers the procedures, results, and theoretical implications of current research in particle physics.

Walker, J. Samuel. *Three Mile Island: A Nuclear Crisis in Historical Perspective*. University of California Press, 2004. The author is the historian of the Nuclear Regulatory Commission and has a thoroughly researched view of the events leading up to—and subsequent to—the accident.

Wolfson, Richard. *Nuclear Choices: A Citizen's Guide to Nuclear Technology*. Cambridge, Mass.: MIT Press, 1993. Written for college-level students, the book is not overwhelmingly advanced but rather provides clear explanations of nuclear technology that includes coverage of the political and social implications of nuclear energy.

Web Sites

Web Sites

The following list contains a sample of sites on the World Wide Web that are relevant to the topic of nuclear energy and high energy particle research. Government agencies engaged in nuclear research can be accessed simply by entering their initials. Examples include the Department of Energy (DOE), the Nuclear Regulatory Commission (NRC), the Environmental Protection Agency (EPA), the National Aeronautics and Space Administration (NASA), and the National Science Foundation (NSF). Owing to the nature of the Internet and the rapid changes that occur there, URL's may have changed since this book was published. If so, the site's name or topic can be used as a search term that should lead to alternative sites and links to other relevant information.

Activist Organizations

The Alliance for Nuclear Accountability is a network of 30 peace and environmental groups. Objectives include obtaining better access to Department of Energy programs and procedures. URL: http://www.ananuclear.org.

Citizen Alert is a voluntary organization that seeks citizen participation in the decisions about nuclear waste disposal in Nevada. URL: http://www.citizenalert.org.

Citizens for Nuclear Technology Awareness is an organization that favors nuclear energy and the continued operation of the Savannah River Site, a nuclear material production facility. URL: http://www.c-n-t-a.com/home.html.

ECOLOGIA is an organization that grew out of the Clamshell Alliance, the citizen's group that attempted to prevent the construction and operation of the Seabrook, New Hampshire, nuclear power plant. ECOLOGIA is now international in scope and provides support to many projects such as nuclear cleanup efforts in the countries of the former Soviet Union. URL: http://www.ecologia/about/index.html.

Nevadans for Nuclear Safety and Benefits is a group that supports the development of the Yucca Mountain site for high-level waste storage. URL: http://www.nnsb.org.

Nevada Nuclear Waste Task Force is a citizen group that opposes the use of the Yucca Mountain site for nuclear waste disposal. URL: http://www.nvantinuclear.org.

The Nuclear Policy Research Institute favors a nuclear-free world and provides a voice for this view through the mass media. URL: http://www.nuclearpolicy.org.

International and Governmental Organizations

The International Atomic Energy Administration is part of the United Nations Organization and is responsible for monitoring international agreements on nuclear testing and nonproliferation. URL: http://www.iaea.org.

The National Nuclear Security Administration is part of the U.S. Department of Energy and supports international programs to prevent the spread of nuclear weapons. They also help gather and securely store obsolete weapon materials. URL: http://www.nnsa.doe.gov.

The Office of Defense–Nuclear Nonproliferation is part of the U. S. Department of Energy and is responsible for monitoring health risks from the handling of nuclear materials and inspections for nuclear disarmament agreements. URL: http://www.nn.doe.gov.

Proliferation Prevention and Arms Control is a unit of the Lawrence Livermore National Laboratory that develops detectors and monitors seismic activity worldwide. URL: http://www.llnl.gov/nai/ppac/ctbt.html.

Professional Organizations

The American Institute of Physics is a collective of specialized professional societies and enrolls physicists in all subfields. The organization publishes *Physics Today,* a magazine geared to students and nonspecialists. URL: http://www. aip.org/aip.

The American Nuclear Society's membership is mainly engineers and researchers in applied fields such as electric power generation and nuclear medicine. The site provides current event information on these topics. URL: http://www. ans.org.

Public Policy Monitors

The Belfer Center for Science and International Affairs is a part of Harvard's Kennedy School of Government. The Center mounts various research programs such as the International Security Program in which arms control procedures are studied. URL: http://bcsia.ksg.harvard.edu.

Bulletin of the Atomic Scientists was founded by a group of physicists who pioneered fission research at the University of Chicago in the 1940s. The group strongly advocates arms control and nuclear disarmament. URL: http://www.the bulletin.org/index.html.

The Carnegie Endowment for Inter-national Peace is a non-profit center that promotes international cooperation. URL: http://www.carnegieendowment.org.

Research Organizations

The Department of Electrical Engineering and Computer Science, Massachusetts Institute of Technology, undertakes research on nuclear fusion and on magnetism using super-conducting materials. URL: http://www.eecs.mit.edu/grad/areaiv.html.

The Infrared Processing and Analysis Center at the California Institute of Technology specializes in studies of infrared radiation from outer space. URL: http://www.ipac.caltech.edu.

The Joint Institute for Nuclear Research is an organization based in Russia that provides a base for cooperative research projects among scientists from Eastern Block nations and provides a linkage to CERN, the European Research Consortium. URL: http://www.jinr.dubna.su.

The Physics Department at Laurentian University in Canada supports studies of reactor design and nuclear waster management at the undergraduate level. URL: http://www.laurentian.ca.

The Physics Department at Boston University gives students the opportunity to study high energy particle physics. URL: http://www.bu.edu.

Index

Italic page numbers indicate illustrations.

A

actinium 15–16
AEC (Atomic Energy Commission) 71, 95
air, supersaturated, in cloud chamber 137
aircraft, nuclear propulsion systems for 88–89
aircraft carriers, nuclear 91
Alamagordo, New Mexico 58–61
Alfred E. Sloan Foundation 179
alpha particles
  in cosmic rays 170
  energy required to create 26
  gold foil irradiated by 20–22, *21*
  nitrogen bombarded with 19
  properties of 17
alpha rays, discovery of 16
aluminum, positron radiation induced in 28
amber, static electricity in 2
ampere 4
Ampère, André-Marie 4
Anderson, Carl 26, 139, 169–170

Annan, Scotland 98
antiatom 139–140, 152–153
antimatter, synthesis of 152–153
antiparticles 162, xiii
Apache Point Observatory (New Mexico) 179
Argonne National Laboratory 74–75, 92, 157–158, *160*
Armed Forces Special Weapons Project 71
arms control 115–116
army, in nuclear weapons development 48
astronomy research, at FermiLab 157
atom
  ancient concepts of 1, xi
  Bohr model of 22–23
  chemical properties of 5
  of gas 4–5
  negative charge in 11
  positive charge in 11
  as scientific theory 1
  solar system analogy of 22, *23*
  spaces between 22
  structure of 20–22, *22–23*, 76

atomic bomb, science necessary for 87. *See also* fission; plutonium bomb; uranium bomb
Atomic Energy Commission (AEC) 71, 95
Atomic Energy Research Establishment (Britain) 80
atomic science, growth of xi
atomic weight 5, 28
Atoms for Peace xii
atom smasher 26–27

B

BaBar 161
barium, in uranium ore 15
Barnwell disposal facility 128
Batavia, Illinois 156
Battelle Memorial Institute 78, 154
battery, in nuclear propulsion system 91
Becquerel, Antoine-Henri 10, 102, *103*
Bell Laboratories, Inc., Sandia National Laboratories managed by 73

197